Shattered
BUT NOT BROKEN

Shattered BUT NOT BROKEN

A Doctor's Transformational
Journey From Illness to Resilience

Kina Peppers, MD, FACOG

publish your gift

SHATTERED BUT NOT BROKEN
Copyright © 2022 Kina Peppers
All rights reserved.

Published by Publish Your Gift®
An imprint of Purposely Created Publishing Group, LLC

No part of this book may be reproduced, distributed or transmitted in any form by any means, graphic, electronic, or mechanical, including photocopy, recording, taping, or by any information storage or retrieval system, without permission in writing from the publisher, except in the case of reprints in the context of reviews, quotes, or references.

Scriptures marked KJV are taken from the Holy Bible, King James Version. All rights reserved.

Printed in the United States of America

ISBN: 978-1-64484-558-5 (print)
ISBN: 978-1-64484-559-2 (ebook)

Special discounts are available on bulk quantity purchases by book clubs, associations and special interest groups. For details email: sales@publishyourgift.com or call (888) 949-6228.
For information log on to www.PublishYourGift.com

Dedication

I dedicate this book to my mom, Pat. Because of your faith, love, and support, I am still here today. Words cannot express my love for you. Thank you for molding my environment and exposing me to a world outside of our neighborhood. You were always my advocate and made sure every test was done to improve my quality of care and saved my life. You taught me to believe in myself and never accept no for an answer.

My sister, Kim, has always been by my side loving me unconditionally. Your remarkable memory reminds me of everything from childhood, even when you were in utero. Our love is everlasting.

Thank you to my best friends, Sylvia, Tracey, Joanne, Bianca, and Joi. We have spent between twenty-one and forty-one years together. Thank you for taking shifts to be by my bedside throughout my journey with the brain aneurysm and neuromyelitis optica.

I thank God who told me that it was not my time yet and gave me the tenacity to learn to walk again, amplified my voice when I could not talk, and restored my sight when doctors said it might not happen.

"I can do all things through Christ which strengtheneth me."—Philippians 4:13 KJV

Table of Contents

Introduction 1

Chapter 1: Everything Was Going So Well 7

Chapter 2: Fighting Wars 21

Chapter 3: When the Unthinkable Happened 29

Chapter 4: Breaking the Chains of Obesity 39

Chapter 5: Releasing the Weight 53

Chapter 6: Being More Intentional 75

Chapter 7: Self-Love: The Change Begins with You 91

Chapter 8: The Way to Go 103

Chapter 9: Welcome to the Winner's Circle 129

Chapter 10: Who's in Your Corner? 133

Chapter 11: Phenomenally YOU 137

Conclusion 141

References 149

About the Author 153

Introduction

"Now faith is the substance of things hoped for, the evidence of things not seen."—Hebrews 11:1 (KJV)

I've experienced great triumphs in my lifetime—triumphs like surviving a severe brain aneurysm, overcoming blindness, overcoming paralysis, and regaining the ability to talk. With every challenge, I focused on the most important life lesson that my mom taught me as a young girl. Mom said, "Don't be defeated by the hand dealt to you. Instead, be victorious despite the attacks and odds." She added, "Life is a new journey each day, and the journey is worth living it." This book has lived inside of me for many years and was finally written with high hopes of helping and inspiring you. Beating the odds and overcoming the challenges listed above required a dedicated focus on my mindset and lifestyle. My personal mantra, *The Cure When There is No Cure*™, has helped me to move beyond my diagnoses to enjoying my life to the fullest. If you are facing a severe or chronic illness, know that you, too, can live better with an illness that may or may not be with you for the rest of your life.

I grew up in a loving, supporting family where we ate well-balanced meals, which included fresh vegetables and lots of fruit. Fast food restaurants like McDonald's were a rare treat. My sister and I were very active with dancing, swimming, track, and gymnastics. As I think back, those were carefree, active, and healthy times. More importantly, those times formed building blocks that would enable me to thrive while living with chronic illnesses. My patients and I speak often about mindful eating and movement being connected to achieving and maintaining a healthy weight needed to help battle illness. As we age, our metabolism slows down, and it becomes more difficult to lose weight and maintain a healthy weight. As both a practicing clinician and patient, I've been on both sides, so I understand and can relate to your journey. I hope my story will help change your mindset in favor of living healthier and overcoming challenges related to living well with chronic illnesses. I have fought my way back from two autoimmune illnesses with tenacity and belief remembering that "…faith is the substance of things hoped for and the evidence of things not seen."

Weight gain is a concern for many women and has become very common. Not only is it frustrating, but significant weight gain can also be depressing, especially when it doesn't respond to your efforts to lose it. There are many triggers for weight gain: stress, chronic illnesses, nutrition, lack of sleep, medications, genetics, your upbringing, yo-yo diets, and more. We'll discuss these triggers and how to best manage them throughout the book. Please know, there were times when I was placed on high doses of steroids to halt the inflammation in my body. As a result, I gained a tremendous amount of weight, making me unrecognizable even to people who'd known me my entire life. Going up five dress sizes in a matter of two months took a major toll on my mental, emotional, and physical health outlook. I was determined to shed the extra pounds and regain my strength and defensive advantage.

I believe that excessive stress, on top of biological predispositions, can send our bodies into haywire. When my brain was attacked by illness, even my memory was affected and I was horrified. During that recovery, I realized that being proactive in my health journey was my best line of defense. It's very similar to a country protecting its territory. It wouldn't be wise to wait until an attack occurs to begin training your military. The troops must be preemptively trained, armed, and ready. Our bodies require the same training and preparation, which is one of the main reasons my body was able to recover after being diagnosed with a second rare autoimmune illness that initially crippled me.

It is only by faith that I have been able to make it through experiences in the Army National Guard, medical school, residency, serving in the Red Zone of Iraq, and debilitating autoimmune illnesses. Many people, even some in my own family, doubted that I could overcome my health challenges or accomplish my dreams. Despite the naysayers, it was faith that just seemed to ground me and propel me to achieve every victory. I also realized that I had a deeper calling. Yes, becoming a physician was part of the calling. However, while serving in Iraq, I was called to perform within and beyond the scope of my specialty. That, too, was part of my calling and preparation for this important assignment.

I realize that I am the sum of every challenge and triumph. Without the challenges, I simply would not be the woman I am today. I am a woman of great faith who continues pushing beyond perceived limits to live the happiest and healthiest life possible. It would be my heart's joy to help you become all that you were meant to be. Over the years, I have gathered tools that I used to pull myself through these experiences and would like to share them through a coaching program designed for women like you who are ready to live their best lives. My program is for women like you who understand that health is wealth. More importantly, it's for women who've been diagnosed with a chronic illness. But it's also for women who, like the military, wish to prepare and train their minds and bodies even without illness. Everyone can benefit from this wellness program because it is customized to your individual journey because no two people are alike.

This book is the manifestation of my calling and preparation. I'm simply sharing a peek into what's possible to prove the power of the mind and resilience of the body. When you put the two together, anything is possible. Remember, it all works together: your habits, relationships, career, emotions, meals, movement (or lack thereof), genetics, and more. It all plays a role in how you show up—mentally, emotionally, and physically.

My faith was instrumental in my efforts to fight through each step forward. Perhaps your battle may be like mine where some days are relatively calm, like gentle waves on the water before a storm. While there will be challenging days, it's important to know that the storm does not last forever. Everyone wants to be healthy. I don't think anyone intends to be unhealthy, but this wellness journey will require change. I pray that while reading these pages, you become even more aware that your body is sacred. Your body is your temple, and it may be time for a makeover. Trust me when I say that what you eat and how you live can impact your ability to get through various health challenges. Therefore, you must be intentional about change. Creating new intentions for your life requires motivation. I hope that this book motivates you to take the first step toward what you thought was impossible. Don't look back—your new life is waiting. If you see yourself in my story, just know that I can help take you to the next level. As Les Brown says, "I aspire, to inspire, until I expire."

I named this book *Shattered but Not Broken* because when you receive shattering news of a devastating diagnosis that may attack your mind, body, or spirit, you may initially feel shattered, but you are *not* broken. I'm ready to help you navigate through and out of the valley to the mountaintop of victory. If you are ready to claim the victory, let's get started!

CHAPTER 1

Everything Was Going So Well

I grew up on Chicago's Southside in a neighborhood of working-class families that still had a village approach, meaning most people knew their neighbors. It was full of kids, so we had plenty of playmates. My parents divorced when my sister and I were just in grammar school, so my mother was a single parent. However, my sister and I weren't at all deprived of love or other necessities. In fact, love and support overflowed in our home. My mother was adamant about her girls growing up in a nurturing environment. We were always encouraged to aim for the stars, to follow our dreams, and to be all we were meant to be. We were witnesses to my mother's refusal to give up no matter the battle. Without a shadow of a doubt, my mother was (and still is) the most ambitious and tenacious person I know.

When I was five, my mother went back to college in pursuit of becoming a registered nurse. To make it all happen—raising two girls, studying to be a nurse, and clocking in at what felt like fifty different jobs—my mother moved us into the first-floor unit at my retired grandparent's home. So, although my sister and I were technically raised by a single mother, we had a village right in our home. This gave us a solid foundation and a level of family support that was invaluable.

My mother, sister, and I did our homework together at our dining room table. I'd be so interested in what my mom was doing that I would hardly be able to focus on my own homework, especially when she brought home this huge cat. I wanted to know all about the heart and all the various organs. I later dissected a frog, labeled all of the organs, and won first place at the science fair. It sparked my desire to become a nurse. I remember telling my mom at some point, "I want to be a nurse just like you." Without hesitation, she responded, "No, sweetheart, you don't want to be the one getting the orders, you want to be the one giving the orders. I want the two of you to go higher than I was able to go." It had always been a dream of mine to be a doctor. She always said to follow your dreams and be the best at whatever you do.

My mom worked multiple jobs while she was in school, so she juggled a lot of balls at once. She always found fun things to do with us, while never missing any of our activities. Some of my favorite memories include the three of us riding our bikes along the lakefront. I even think that may be one of the reasons I love running on the lakefront today. I thought my mother was a super woman who had superpowers and could walk into a telephone booth, turn around, and then step out with a cape. I thought she was the goddess of everything. To this day, I do not feel there is anything, if she sets her mind to it, that she cannot do. "Cannot" was not and is not part of her vocabulary then or today.

During grammar school, my granddad would cook us breakfast every morning. He always asked what we wanted, and actually made it. My grandparents were originally from Alabama, so we grew up experiencing a lot of southern mannerisms and even more southern meals. For instance, for breakfast, he enjoyed making homemade pancakes and biscuits, eggs, bacon, salt pork, sausage, grits, and more. When the food was ready, he would ring a cowbell that he brought from his farm in Alabama, and that was our signal to come upstairs and eat.

After breakfast, he would then make sure we made it to school safely by either walking us to the bus stop or riding the bus with us to school. Occasionally, he'd even show up at the school and ride the bus home with us too. The kids on the bus loved my grandaddy too because he'd bring enough candy for everyone.

My mom worked extra jobs as an emergency room nurse to afford tuition for Catholic grammar and high school. She made sure our minds and bodies stayed active too. She wanted us to be well-rounded young women, so she created our environment. Between grammar school and high school, we took swimming lessons, track and field, ballet, piano lessons, tennis, gymnastics, and the list goes on. Then we'd come home and play with our friends on the block. Double Dutch, dodgeball, softball, hopscotch, racing (none of the girls could outrun me, so I only raced the boys), you name the game and we probably played it.

I graduated high school, and I headed off to college. Although I received some scholarships and grants, it was not enough pay for everything. My mother was still working overtime to help pay for my college tuition and fees, just as she'd done for me and my sister back in our Catholic school days. During my second year of college, a recruiter from the Army National Guard visited our campus. He said that I could get a 100 percent scholarship and a monthly stipend if I went to a state-funded college. I wanted to relieve my mother from having to work so hard to help pay my tuition for college, so the National Guard sounded like the perfect solution.

In 1987, I joined the Illinois Army National Guard as a Private First Class, then decided I wanted to become an officer in 1991. I was recommended amongst several hundreds of other eager soldiers throughout the state to become a competitor for Officer Candidate School. In my mind, it was what my mom had told me before: "You don't want to be the one that's taking the orders. You want to be the one that's giving the orders." So, I wanted to become an officer. One of my sergeants doubted that I'd be able to get through it, because, according to him, I didn't like anyone telling me what to do. I told him, "I'm going to make it. I'm going to do it." There were hundreds of people who had been nominated by the top officers in their companies. We went through this lengthy process of getting chosen for Officer Candidate School. We started out with a class of one-hundred thirty, and eighteen months later we graduated a class of twenty-nine. I was at the top of my class with only four other female candidates becoming a fresh second lieutenant.

This was a huge milestone for me, as it was very mentally and physically challenging. After being told by the training officers that I'd never become one of them, I made every stride and never gave up. My mother always told me that when someone says you can't, you prove them wrong by showing them that you can. I did just that. It was purely mind over matter. Low crawling in mud, push-ups and pull-ups, and five-mile runs to prepare us. If you had to vomit, they'd tell you to throw up over your shoulder and keep running. The whole time, they'd be in your face telling you that you can't do it. I was in shape, so I was very capable, but it was still extremely difficult. It was a test to your mind and your body. It was warrior training in every sense of the word.

I worked in the medical unit during that time as a patient administrator. When I got back to the unit, I saw the sergeant who'd first told me that I wouldn't be able to do it. I called him out on it too. "Remember you told me I wouldn't be able to make it?" I asked him. He snapped to attention, threw his arm up, saluted me, and said, "Yes, ma'am." From that point on, that's how he addressed me. I earned my respect, which was hard for *anyone* to do in the military back then, *especially* women. It wasn't in my blood to give up though. After all, I was raised by a super woman.

After graduating from college, I was accepted to medical school and received the Illinois Department of Public Health Scholarship, which paid 100 percent tuition with a monthly stipend. Upon graduating from medical school, I was the first in my family to become a doctor. My mother was in the hospital for major surgery when it was time for me to graduate, and she demanded to be discharged. She told the doctors that she would sign an against medical advice (AMA) form so that she could see her baby walk across the stage, but she didn't have to. Her surgeon discharged her a day early. Like any other parent in her predicament, she wanted to be present to witness this proud moment, and for her, it was worth any risk and sacrifice.

Following graduation, I matched high on my list into an OBGYN residency program, was intern of the year, and was selected as chief resident in my fourth year. Things seemed great, right?

Wrong.

In October, during my second year of residency, I began having strange neurologic symptoms: painful prickly, burning sensations in my legs, arms, and hands and then all over my body. It felt like some was sticking all over with pins. After seeing a neurologist, I was told my CT scan was abnormal with a plan for a follow up MRI. A few days later I was on call at the hospital, and I started feeling feverish with a headache. Once I made it home my headache intensified, my temperature was 103 degrees, and I started taking Tylenol every four hours, but there was no improvement. I was taken to the emergency room, and in the era of the West Nile Virus, I was given a spinal tap and admitted. Unable to get my temperature down, I had to have cooling blankets applied. Every lymph node in my body was inflamed, my organs started to fail, and I had swelling in my brain. I was transferred to the intensive care unit and started on high doses of steroids. They thought they were going to have to take out my gallbladder at one point. I remember the neurologist coming into the room and saying, "We have to save her brain." That's when they started me on massive doses of IV steroids. I was diagnosed with an autoimmune disorder, Sjogren's

Syndrome. The usual age of someone being affected with this autoimmune condition usually affects people over forty years of age, but it is believed my first attack was at the age of seventeen, and misdiagnosed. My symptoms improved on steroids, and I was eventually discharged home, but I was told I may not be able to finish residency.

A couple of months later, my father, who had been diagnosed with lung cancer that had spread to his liver and brain, was placed on home hospice. My sister and I spent that Christmas morning with our father and stepmom and then went back home to have dinner with our mom and family. My mom had been complaining of neck pain that entire day. She has multiple sclerosis, so the pain could have easily been dismissed as a symptom of that. As we were about to sit down for dinner, my mother screamed, and fell to the floor stating, "I had a very sharp pain in my head, but I'm fine now."

My sister noticed a blank stare on our mom's face at the dinner table and asked if she was okay. Though it wasn't clear or coherent, we made out, "I think I'm having a stroke." We scooped the food out of her mouth, then she went limp. We managed to get her to the floor right before she started having seizures (something she had never had). My brother-in-law, who's a police officer, and his partner came for their dinner break and were present in uniform with their police car. He called for an ambulance from his walkie talkie, and she was rushed to the emergency room.

What we did not know, however, was that our father was also being rushed to another emergency room because he had stopped breathing. He passed that day at another hospital. Because of his declining condition, there were "do not resuscitate" (DNR) orders. We almost lost both of our parents at the same time on the same Christmas day.

The doctors found that my mom had a ruptured brain aneurysm. She'd become paralyzed and was temporarily unable to speak. Not too many people are able to talk about an aneurysm that ruptures, but she was able to. Remarkably, after surgery and rehabilitation, by the grace of God, she had a full recovery.

Well, let's get back to me. All of this occurred between October and December. The steroids added seventy pounds to my tiny frame. I stopped counting after seventy pounds. I went up five dress sizes. When I ate breakfast, I was trying to figure out what I was eating for lunch. When I had lunch, I was trying to figure out what I was eating for dinner. And when I had dinner, I was trying to figure out the snack I was going to have before I went to bed. Because it was the holiday season, I had to have warmed sweet potato pie or peach cobbler topped with butter pecan ice-cream. It wasn't just a physical reaction; it was mental too. I started having cravings and different eating behaviors.

I gained so much weight that people I knew had difficulty accepting that it was really me. I ran into my first cousin at the hair salon one day. We had grown up together and spent every weekend and summer of our youth together. She did not recognize me, and it made me feel terrible. Nobody knew who I was. It felt like steroids had stolen my identity. That's what I was NOT prepared for. They save your life, but they also change your life. I had what they call a moon face, because your face will literally become round with your cheeks appearing to be blown out and a double chin. I felt like the balloon cartoon character in the Thanksgiving Day parade. One needle and I'd deflate. It did a number on my self-esteem. I had never been on a diet before and had never even really paid attention to what I ate. I very slowly tapered off the steroids, which I felt were taking over my body and my mind.

Everything seemed to be happening at the same time, and it was a lot to process. I had this new diagnosis, and doctors told me they didn't think I'd be able to finish my residency. Sjogren's is normally associated with a dry mouth and dry eyes. Those are symptoms too, but there is so much more to Sjogren's. There's a neurologic component, which is what I experienced. My entire body felt like an enormous cushion with all kinds of pins and needles sticking me constantly. In addition to living with a new autoimmune illness and going through recovery, I was also adjusting to my new body weight while mourning my father and worrying about my mother.

I didn't know if I was going to return to normal or if this was my new normal. I didn't know what the future held for me. But I knew that my grandfather was a reverend and my whole family was very prayerful. I read a quote online recently that said, "Your grandmother's prayers are still protecting you." Not only do I believe that, but I'm also a witness to it. I knew that God did not bring me this far to leave me like this, and I also knew that faith without works is dead.

Months later, I was able to return to my residency program and resumed my studies. Even though I was welcomed back with cheers, I felt the stares and heard whispers behind my back. My appearance had changed drastically, and I was unrecognizable to many of my follow doctors because of the change in my appearance, but I was there! The weight was very uncomfortable to carry. I moved slower and had some shortness of breath.

That day when I returned home, I did something I had been avoiding for months, and that was looking in the mirror. I was borrowing my mom's clothes (size 12 and 14) and knew I was gaining weight because I had worn a size 4 before Sjogren's. Until this day, I had been in denial, but as I looked in the mirror, the tears began running down my face as I stood before the mirror I had been avoiding for weeks. On this day, I made a commitment to take back control of my body, my mind, and how I would live my life.

Together with some of my closest friends in residency, we organized a weight loss challenge as a coping mechanism to help lose the pounds and change our mindset. We started cardio and strength training as well as meal prepping. Everybody put money in so that the person who lost the most weight would get the winning pot at the end. We even supported each other at the gym doing workouts. Between the accountability factor and the money motivation, it worked for my comrades and me. It was incredible and so extremely helpful. While we had been in residency, we mostly ate in the hospital's cafeteria. Whatever they served is what we ate, and the choices usually weren't very healthy. I quickly realized that if I wanted to turn my situation around, then I had to make some lifestyle changes too. Once I made that decision, every piece of food that I put in my mouth came out of my pre-packed lunch bag. Throughout my four years of residency, we grew very close and supported one another in our personal and professional lives.

I continued my rehabilitation and weight loss journey. After about twelve weeks off, and despite everything I had gone through, I went back into my residency program and was selected as chief resident in my last year. I was able to finish my residency with my class in June of 2005. Through meal prepping, cardio, and strength training, I eventually regained my strength and shed some of those unwanted pounds. Seventy plus pounds was a lot to lose—not easy and not fast. So many factors played a role, including changes in mindset, meditation, affirmations, mindful eating, and journaling. Determination and resilience gave me my life back to enjoy, healthy and in shape.

CHAPTER 2

Fighting Wars

Within one year of completing residency and receiving my license to practice medicine, I was deployed to Iraq as part of my Army National Guard duty. As a resident, I was still in training, so I was not eligible to be deployed. Once I became a fully licensed physician, I became eligible and was deployed six months later. At this time, my Sjogren's was under control, and the Army considered me fit for duty. They made sure I had my medication and was able to be deployed with everyone else. This was difficult for me, considering everything I'd gone through to get to this point, and it was also hard on my family. We are a praying family, so we stayed grounded in our faith and knew that if God had brought me through all the other battles, He was not about to forsake me now.

We started our journey on a commercial flight in the United States but changed to a military transport aircraft to fly into Iraq. Soldiers don't fly onto the military base in a regular airplane. There are no flight attendants walking around giving snacks and beverages. There aren't any buttons to recline your seat or pillows to make the ride more comfortable. You are sitting on a webbed seat with a crisscross material and a seatbelt. At the end of an exceptionally long, monotonous flight, our plane suddenly began plummeting toward the ground. We thought the plane was crashing. Everyone was praying. Some people were throwing up into their helmets, and some were screaming. This must have been everyone's first time flying on a military airplane onto a base in a war zone. A moment later, the plane had safely landed on the ground. I didn't know if I needed to get off the plane with my weapon drawn, because we all at this point had weapons with ammunition. I didn't know if I needed to lock and load my nine-millimeter, drop and roll, then start shooting. Once we exited the plane, we found out that they did what was called a combat landing to avoid getting shot out of the sky.

I worked at what's called a Troop Medical Clinic (TMC) where we saw patients who had primary issues: high blood pressure, diabetes, asthma, and more. These individuals may have already been on medication or were diagnosed with a new illness. It was basically like I was a primary care physician. We also saw patients with bumps and bruises or colds and sniffles and those who had been injured in combat, but whose wounds were not severe enough to require going to the hospital. The base on which I was stationed was the only military "trauma hospital" in Iraq. We were responsible for removing shrapnel from someone's legs or face, readjusting dislocated shoulders, and so much more. I worked in a Women's Health Clinic and was also on the sexual assault team, as sexual assault unfortunately occurs in war zones. I carried a pager for the trauma hospital, which was for them to alert me that a gynecology emergency surgery patient was arriving by helicopter or that my assistance was needed. There were women who were bleeding out from a miscarriage or an ectopic pregnancy who were my responsibility, as I was the only OBGYN on the base.

When my pager went off, I would head to the trauma hospital in full combat gear. Because I am a licensed surgeon, my assistance was often needed in the operating room. Even if they are not trained in a particular specialty, licensed surgeons are qualified to be the main surgeon's assistant. With direction and guidance, I may have been working with a vascular or trauma surgeon or any other type of specialist. Ambulances and helicopters arrived all day and night bringing soldiers, civilian contractors, and Iraqi prisoners in from the field to the trauma hospital.

I felt the ground shake from explosions more times than I can count and really learned how to work through pressure and fear. We'd hear a *boom*, the building would shake, and the lights would flicker. Everyone looked up at each other, then we went right back to operating as if nothing happened. It was a life-changing experience. I wouldn't do anything differently, even if I could.

I wore all those different hats while I was there, so I was quite busy. I am so honored to have my contributions acknowledged with the awarding of a Bronze Star. My tour of duty was not easy, but it was worth it was well worth it to help my comrades the best that I knew how. We were all a team. It was not only challenging to my mind and body, but also to my faith and spirit.

We got mortared every single day. They had speakers on the base, and someone would announce over the speakers, "Incoming!" The person making the announcement sounded so distraught that they just made you feel nervous. We had what was called a C-Ram (a counter-rocket, artillery, mortar) that was designed to protect ground forces and bases from the threat of rockets, artillery, and mortars. It would detect incoming missiles then shoot them out of the sky, so they'd explode before hitting the ground. When we heard the Incoming announcement, that was our cue to run to the bunker. This way, you were undercover when it arrived, and you would pray it wouldn't harm or kill you. Everything that I have been through up until now has made me into the woman that I have become.

I did a tour in 2006 and another tour in 2009. Although I knew the military could deploy me as a physician every three years, I was still initially upset about that second tour. I'd just gotten married and was starting to regain my footing and peace of mind being at home from my first tour. I really did not want to return to Iraq again, however, I had no choice. When I got there, I realized that my needing to be there went deeper than I could have ever imagined. I was there to save lives. There was one female civilian contractor, for instance, who presented to the trauma hospital with abdominal pain and a positive pregnancy test. A CT scan was done showing she had blood in her abdomen up to her liver. They were going to put her in a helicopter and send her to Baghdad. I said, "No way, no how!" She had a ruptured ectopic pregnancy and if she had been placed in a helicopter, she would have died.

When I got to the hospital, her hemoglobin was 4, which is extremely low. A normal range is between 12 and 15 for a woman. She had lost a lot of blood into her abdomen from the ectopic pregnancy. When I made that incision to get into her belly, the blood sprouted out like a fountain. When you have ectopic pregnancy, you're in a lot of pain. That pregnancy is not in the uterus, as it should be. Instead, it was in the fallopian tube. The fallopian tube is skinny like a telephone cord. It's not meant for a baby to grow in, so as that baby gets bigger, it ruptures that fallopian tube, and you continue to have active bleeding inside of the abdomen. A ruptured ectopic pregnancy is the number one cause of death in pregnant women. I repaired everything during surgery and made sure she got blood. After that happened, I started getting the emergency gynecology surgeries. It was a blessing because the outcome may not have been as successful if they had to be flown to Baghdad. The second tour was no less dangerous or hectic than the first one.

Prior to my second deployment, I started training for my first Chicago Marathon. It's a big deal, and this would be my first time running it. Iraq was probably not the perfect place to train. The early morning temperature was ninety degrees or higher. I even ran a half-marathon in remembrance of 9/11, with the temperature in Iraq rising to 130 degrees. So, whereas I thought my deployment was the *why*, it turned out to be the *why not*! I was part of a team that again saved lives as well as put me in the position to do something that I'd been wanting to do for a very long time.

I'm a strong believer in accountability. I've witnessed time and time again how powerful that network of support is—in my personal life as well as in the lives of my clients. When I was training for the marathon in Iraq, we were mortared daily and there were times that running outdoors was not feasible, so I started running on the treadmill, which was boring. During a meeting with a General, I discovered there was a group of other women in leadership positions who were running outside. I dropped those fears, and they were running right there beside me. We all had our individual goals, but we figured out a way to make it work for all of us. Because my goal consisted of the longest run, I'd have a group of women run with me for the first five miles, then another group would start for the next five miles, and a third group would run the final stretch with me. Just over 1 week after I returned home, I completed my first Chicago Marathon. I was so elated when a fellow comrade, who was my running buddy in Iraq, surprised me and flew into Chicago from Kentucky to run side by side in the marathon with me.

Motivation is key with marathons because you never train for the entire length of the marathon. The Chicago Marathon is 26.2 miles. The most you might run while training is twenty-one miles. The rest of it is mind over matter—the gut, the intestinal fortitude. Let's back up to training though. Much of preparing for and actually running a marathon comes down to mindset, motivation, using those affirmations. I'd do a short run three days a week and then a long run on Saturdays. It was incredibly challenging. Just as the body gets accustomed to poor habits, it also has a phenomenal way of adapting to positive changes and challenges.

There are a lot of moving parts, however. I wouldn't have made nearly as much progress without the dieting aspect of the journey. Many people get discouraged when they don't see progress, and they don't see progress because they're skipping steps. Your diet and your mindset are key. You must put those affirmations out there. Even if you're only running two miles, tell yourself "I am a runner" and get out there and run. If you're cleaning up your diet, tell yourself "I eat to live." Also know that you can't sit across from people who eat hamburgers and hot wings all day. Talk yourself into meeting the right people. If you're around the right people, you'll succeed. I surrounded myself with runners and other athletes while training for the marathon. That I-can-do-it attitude is contagious, and it'll help you fight the wars without excuses. On top of training in Iraq and Chicago, I was still working. Because I was committed though, I found a way to make it work and stuck with it. The formula worked! The Chicago Marathon was now checked it off my bucket list.

Everything wasn't peaches and cream though. Prior to returning from my second deployment, I developed a thumping in my right ear. It didn't happen all the time—mainly when I was lying down on my right side—but it'd wake me out of my sleep sometimes. Even though this was not constant, it was frequent enough for me to seek medical advice. I saw a doctor on my base in Iraq about this issue. They did a hearing and an equilibrium test, but they could not figure out what was wrong.

CHAPTER 3

When the Unthinkable Happened

Life was going so well. I returned home after two tours in Iraq's red zone and completed two Chicago Marathons. The last one I ran was in October of 2012 with dedication, training, perseverance, and a can-do mindset. I ran every half marathon, ten-miler, and even 5K leading up to this event and finished thanking God for giving me the strength to make it through.

I worked for five years in an "underserved area" to give back to the Illinois Department of Public Health Scholarship which paid for medical school and gave me a monthly stipend. This scholarship only required four years of giving back, but since so much was given to me, I wanted to give more, which I did, and worked an extra year.

I was offered and received a dream job with a prestigious women's group here in Chicago with all the bells and whistles, which included a significant raise in salary. All was going well. I had a beautiful duplex condo, a loving husband, and a new job, and we were again planning a family.

But after only one year at my new job, the unthinkable started to unfold. The thumping in my right ear began escalating to the point that I didn't have to be lying down to hear the thumping. It bothered me throughout the day, even while I was standing. I went to see a neurologist two months later, and she decided to send me for a magnetic resonance angiography (MRA). The results of the MRA were devastating news—they which showed an unusual aneurysm on the left side of my brain. These findings were what are called "incidental findings," completely unrelated to the thumping in my right ear. But that's not the end to my story, just another new beginning that spiraled down a pathway towards my destiny—another testing of my resilience and faith.

I was seen by a specialist, but no one could diagnose what was wrong. This finding was only two months after running the marathon. The doctor surmised that if the MRA had not been ordered, the aneurysm might have ruptured without any symptoms. In case you aren't familiar, aneurysms occur when part of an artery wall gets weak and begins to expand like a balloon. This causes the artery walls to become thin enough to rupture. If that happens, then there becomes an issue of internal bleeding in the brain, the risk of a stroke, and even death.

It just so happened that the brain aneurysm that I had was on the opposite side of the brain. The thumping was in the right ear, and the brain aneurysm was on the left side of my brain. It had absolutely nothing to do with the thumping in the right ear. Had it not been for the ear thumping, I would not have had the MRA done. As was the case with my mother, aneurysms often have no signs or symptoms until they rupture.

When my mom's brain aneurysm ruptured, it led to seizures, paralyses, and other complications. She had no indication until she had a pain in her head that felt like a bomb exploding. Because of what I witnessed my mother, I wanted to hopefully avoid the same thing happening to me, so I opted for immediate surgery. The doctor said it was the worst aneurysm he'd ever repaired, and it was a blessing that the aneurysm did not rupture while I was running the marathon two months prior. The weakened area of the aneurysm branched out like a spider as it tried to supply blood to other areas of my brain. So, when the brain surgeon started the surgery, he had to remove a section of my skull to be able to go directly into my brain. He had to dig deeper into my brain than originally anticipated in order to get to the base of the aneurysm.

My family and friends thought that I hadn't made it through surgery. They misread the look on my neurosurgeon's face when he came out to share the complications of the long, intense surgery. I didn't wake up for days, had seizures every two to three minutes for fourteen hours because of brain manipulation, and had some residual bleeding during the surgery. My speech was jumbled, I had difficulty seeing, short-term memory loss, and trouble walking. I could not even remember my name. One of the treatments used was steroids to help with the brain swelling, which assisted in my gaining more than forty pounds. I had countless hours of speech, occupational, physical, and cognitive therapy, which challenged my faith and mindset to say the least. I had to learn to walk again, which the doctors were not sure I would. However, my mother would not allow the doctors to speak negativity to me. I learned to speak again and to do many other simple things, which included cooking and combing my hair. I was determined to fight and always pushed further than I was instructed to because of my faith, tenacity, and saying to myself, "I can do all things through Christ which strengthens me" (Philippians 4:13, KJV). I am blessed to have made a full recovery.

I got through it and started back on a healthy diet, running, cross fit, high-intensity interval training (HIIT), and yoga. Again, I rise! I knew that I was a walking miracle and believed in the power of perseverance. Everyone who knew the story was in complete awe. A friend of mine who heard about my story was associated with a syndicated talk show called *The Doctors* and told the producers of my story. They interviewed me over the phone then came to my home to film and talk to my husband, mother, and one of my best friends. I was then invited to go to Los Angeles to share my story on the show. I initially turned them down, but my friend would come back and ask again from time to time. I did not think I was ready to tell the story without sobbing. But two years later, I decided it was time to share my story because it might help someone else. I flew out to Los Angeles to appear on *The Doctors* to inspire other people who have been through a brain aneurysm or any other medical illnesses, and doing this also helped me to let others in. It was such an awesome show and experience that when I returned to Chicago, I accepted the invitation to do three local news shows.

Everything was going so well, I had recently joined a new private practice group, and the second of the three local shows aired on a Monday. But by that weekend, the unthinkable happened again. I began experiencing intractable hiccups with nausea and vomiting. After being admitted to the hospital, I quickly deteriorated with difficulty breathing and was placed on a ventilator and put in a medically induced coma in the neuro-intensive care unit for two weeks.

Once I was weaned from the breathing machine, I could hear footsteps in my room and voices of my loved ones and doctors, but I could only see intermittent grey as they walked by. I could feel a draft as the sheets were pulled off my legs and I was asked to move my feet. I remember thinking, "Of course I can move my feet." After trying, however, I realized that I couldn't. I tried to answer them, but no one could hear my voice. They'd have to put their ear to my lips. The neuromyelitis optica (NMO) paralyzed my body, and the intubation paralyzed my vocal cord. NMO is a rare autoimmune disease that only affects four thousand people in the United States. Many NMO-related deaths are due to respiratory failure. The labs sent out confirmed my diagnosis and the MRI showed lesions along my cervical spine with swelling in my brain. As the adage says best, "It could be much worse." If I had not been admitted for the hiccups, I would have stopped breathing and had no one around me to help. God brought me into that hospital. Mind you, I wasn't short of breath when I got to the hospital. I became short of breath while I was there, so they were fortunately able to almost immediately intubate me and put me on life support. Right place at the right time.

There was no jumping out of the bed to run downstairs or to start a run. On top of having no muscle control—having to be turned in the bed to be cleaned or dressed—I couldn't even see. No looking at my loved ones, seeing flowers bloom, or watching the sun rise or set.

There's always something to be grateful for, though. Always. I was in the right place for me to go from the hospital over to rehabilitation to start my physical therapy. I had physical therapy, occupational therapy, speech therapy, and cognitive therapy. Prior to leaving the neuro-intensive unit, I remember my physical therapist sitting me up in bed then turning his back for two seconds. I immediately fell forward because I had no muscle tone. He then placed my arms around his neck, which didn't stay, and he lifted me up. My legs dangled like a raggedy Anne doll. Pillows had to be placed at my sides to keep me upright and the chair had to be tilted to keep my head up. The absolute hardest thing I've ever done, however, was learn how to walk again. I'd do so from a machine picking me up with my toes barely touching the ground, to hanging from a harness from the ceiling.

Although it was hard, I did it! I vowed to never give up on myself. Not once. Even after the doctors said it was a strong possibility that I'd never walk again or regain my vision, by the grace of God, I did! Once again, I persevered. Through rehabilitation and resilience and with a positive mindset and motivation, I learned to walk again, regained my vision, and shed the unwanted thirty pounds from massive steroids. The physical therapist was in awe. He said because I was in great shape prior to my diagnosis, muscle memory played a role in my recovery. So, what I did (exercise, nutrition, etc.) prior to my illness as well as after I was hospitalized played a major part in my healing. Being both proactive in your health, and when necessary, reactive, is the key! Proactivity was the running, training, and meal-prepping. Being reactive to the illnesses included the surgeries; steroids; and cognitive, occupational, and physical therapy. All are critical. Equal to the physical commitment, however, is the mental and spiritual work.

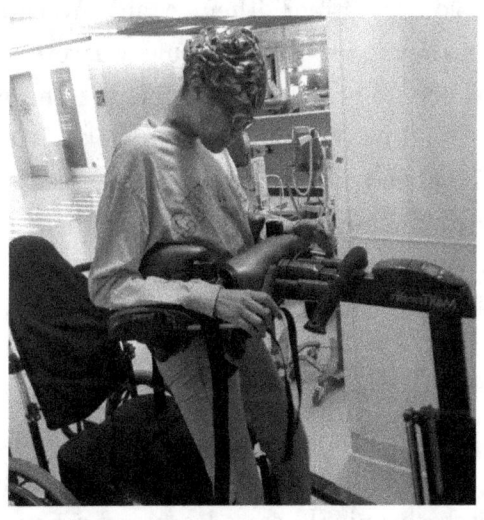

Recently, I had a doctor's appointment at the same hospital to which I was admitted with these life-altering events. When I exited the elevator, I ran into the neuro-ophthalmologist who took care of me when I was blind. I called his name, reintroduced myself, and told him he may not remember me and explained how I saw him while blind and in rehabilitation after diagnosis of neuromyelitis optica. He literally finished telling me my story and as if it happened yesterday although it was seven years prior. He remembered all of the specifics, including my history of Sjogren's, my brain aneurysm, and my working at that hospital. The doctor then peppered me with questions. "Are you still receiving chemotherapy? How is your vision? You are walking without assistance? Are you able to work? Are you operating?" Then he said, "You are blessed, and God has a plan for you". Although we were both wearing masks, I could hear the astonishment in his voice and see his mouth drop in disbelief as we spoke. With tears in my eyes, I thanked him for taking great care of me.

When someone says I can't do it or that I might not be able to, my responses are "I will" and "I do." And it's worked, as you'll realize over the course of this book, time and time again. I have been able to take each of my own personal health crisis, along with my experience treating others with ailments other than my own and tap into my purpose. As a result, I am now passionate about helping women with chronic illnesses learn and practice healthy habits that improve their quality of life. With my mantra, "The Cure When There is No Cure," at the forefront, I provide a holistic approach to a healthy mindset, diet, and weight loss that promotes physical, mental, emotional, and spiritual wellness.

CHAPTER 4

Breaking the Chains of Obesity

Let's chat about your weight assessment. It's just not that simple!

Is your weight normal, overweight, or obese? What are the risk factors for obesity?

In June 2013, the American Medical Association (AMA) House of Delegates voted to recognize obesity as a disease state requiring treatment and prevention efforts. It's not just a poor lifestyle choice. Obesity is estimated to cause approximately 112,000 to 365,000 deaths per year.

Weight and health risk assessment involves three measurements

- Body Mass Index (BMI) to classify obesity
- Waist circumference
- Disease or comorbidities that are increased because of obesity

Body Mass Index

Obesity is a compounded medical condition that's more than weight gain. Definitions for overweight and obesity are universally applied using body mass index and based on morbidity and mortality. There is excess accumulation of fat that alters your health and increases risk factors for life-altering disease.

BMI is a screening tool that is divided up into five categories:

1. Normal Weight
2. Overweight
3. Class I obesity
4. Class II Obesity
5. Class III obesity

BMI = Weight (lb) / [Height (in)]^2 x 703 OR Weight (kg) / [Height (m)]^2

Shattered But Not Broken

Body Mass Index Table

Height (inches)	Normal							Overweight						Obese												Extreme Obesity															
BMI	19	20	21	22	23	24	25	26	27	28	29	30	31	32	33	34	35	36	37	38	39	40	41	42	43	44	45	46	47	48	49	50	51	52	53	54
	Body Weight (pounds)																																			
58	91	96	100	105	110	115	119	124	129	134	138	143	148	153	158	162	167	172	177	181	186	191	196	201	205	210	215	220	224	229	234	239	244	248	253	258
59	94	99	104	109	114	119	124	128	133	138	143	148	153	158	163	168	173	178	183	188	193	198	203	208	212	217	222	227	232	237	242	247	252	257	262	267
60	97	102	107	112	118	123	128	133	138	143	148	153	158	163	168	174	179	184	189	194	199	204	209	215	220	225	230	235	240	245	250	255	261	266	271	276
61	100	106	111	116	122	127	132	137	143	148	153	158	164	169	174	180	185	190	195	201	206	211	217	222	227	232	238	243	248	254	259	264	269	275	280	285
62	104	109	115	120	126	131	136	142	147	153	158	164	169	175	180	186	191	196	202	207	213	218	224	229	235	240	246	251	256	262	267	273	278	284	289	295
63	107	113	118	124	130	135	141	146	152	158	163	169	175	180	186	191	197	203	208	214	220	225	231	237	242	248	254	259	265	270	278	282	287	293	299	304
64	110	116	122	128	134	140	145	151	157	163	169	174	180	186	192	197	204	209	215	221	227	232	238	244	250	256	262	267	273	279	285	291	296	302	308	314
65	114	120	126	132	138	144	150	156	162	168	174	180	186	192	198	204	210	216	222	228	234	240	246	252	258	264	270	276	282	288	294	300	306	312	318	324
66	118	124	130	136	142	148	155	161	167	173	179	186	192	198	204	210	216	223	229	235	241	247	253	260	266	272	278	284	291	297	303	309	315	322	328	334
67	121	127	134	140	146	153	159	166	172	178	185	191	198	204	211	217	223	230	236	242	249	255	261	268	274	280	287	293	299	306	312	319	325	331	338	344
68	125	131	138	144	151	158	164	171	177	184	190	197	203	210	216	223	230	236	243	249	256	262	269	276	282	289	295	302	308	315	322	328	335	341	348	354
69	128	135	142	149	155	162	169	176	182	189	196	203	209	216	223	230	236	243	250	257	263	270	277	284	291	297	304	311	318	324	331	338	345	351	358	365
70	132	139	146	153	160	167	174	181	188	195	202	209	216	222	229	236	243	250	257	264	271	278	285	292	299	306	313	320	327	334	341	348	355	362	369	376
71	136	143	150	157	165	172	179	186	193	200	208	215	222	229	236	243	250	257	265	272	279	286	293	301	308	315	322	329	338	343	351	358	365	372	379	386
72	140	147	154	162	169	177	184	191	199	206	213	221	228	235	242	250	258	265	272	279	287	294	302	309	316	324	331	338	346	353	361	368	375	383	390	397
73	144	151	159	166	174	182	189	197	204	212	219	227	235	242	250	257	265	272	280	288	295	302	310	318	325	333	340	348	355	363	371	378	386	393	401	408
74	148	155	163	171	179	186	194	202	210	218	225	233	241	249	256	264	272	280	287	295	303	311	319	326	334	342	350	358	365	373	381	389	396	404	412	420
75	152	160	168	176	184	192	200	208	216	224	232	240	248	256	264	272	279	287	295	303	311	319	327	335	343	351	359	367	375	383	391	399	407	415	423	431
76	156	164	172	180	189	197	205	213	221	230	238	246	254	263	271	279	287	295	304	312	320	328	336	344	353	361	369	377	385	394	402	410	418	426	435	443

Source: Adapted from Clinical Guidelines on the Identification, Evaluation, and Treatment of Overweight and Obesity in Adults: The Evidence Report.

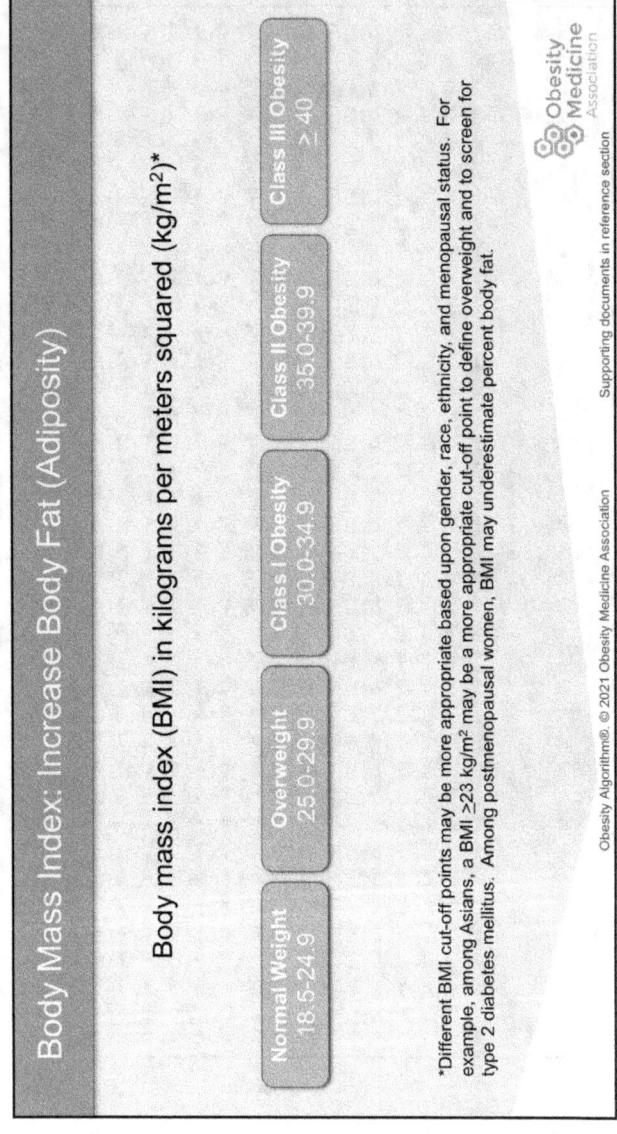

There are some issues with the data because they are based on white European male population.

BMI is an inaccurate measure of body fat (adiposity) content and does not consider variations in muscle mass, bone density, overall body composition, and racial and sex differences. If all of these were constant and only body fat varied, it would capture adiposity. This is what happens when someone has heavier muscle mass and is considered obese by BMI (an overdiagnosis) but their body fat falls in the normal range. The opposite also happens, and obesity can be underdiagnosed in people who have sarcopenia—the loss of muscle mass and function due to aging. Active day-to-day activities may become a problem with the risk of fractures after falling.

Research has shown that blacks and whites and males and females have different body compositions. Therefore, the BMI should be adjusted. There have been adjustments for Asians because at a lower BMI, they have a higher risk of metabolic diseases. Asians may have health problems and be overweight with a BMI greater than 23. Obesity would start with a BMI greater than 27.5. These adjustments have not been made for the black and Latino communities. This has led to a proposed recalibration that was more individualized instead of the "one-size fits all."

TABLE. Cutoffs for BMI Based on ROC Curve Analysis

	BMI (kg/m^2)					
	Men			Women		
Obesity Co-morbidity	Black	Hispanic	White	Black	Hispanic	White
Hypertension	28	29	28	31	28	27
Dyslipidemia	27	26	27	29	27	25
Diabetes	29	29	30	33	30	29
≥2 risk factors	28	29	29	31	30	28
Average	28	28	29	31	29	27

BMI = body mass index; ROC = receiver operating characteristic.

BMI is the standard used in the United States, and physicians typically calculate BMI on all patients. It's usually an automated part of the electronic medical record. Other methods can calculate body fat, and some may be more or less specific. These include waist circumference, which can be used to accompany BMI; skinfold thickness or the pinch test; dual energy X-ray absorptiometry (DEXA scan), which also measures bone density for risk of osteoporosis; hydrostatic weighing; and bio impedance "smart scales." BMI is easily obtainable and can be easily calculated or found on a chart.

According to the National Institute of Health, higher BMI (greater than or equal to 30), increases your risk for certain diseases such as heart disease, high blood pressure, type 2 diabetes, gallstones, breathing problems, and certain cancers, and the recommendation would be weight loss. If you are overweight (BMI of 25 to 29.9) and you have two additional risk factors, weight loss is recommended as well.

Waist Circumference

A large waist circumference is sometimes referred to as abdominal or central obesity. The fat that you can pinch is likely abdominal fat that is subcutaneous and right beneath the skin. Fat that you can't pinch is visceral fat and can wrap around your organs. Imagine two different body types: an apple or a pear. Men commonly have an apple shape, which represenents abdominal obesity. Women tend to pick up weight around their hips and thighs, giving them a pear shape.

While looking in the mirror you may see that the circumference around your waist is more than your hips. Waist circumference in combination with your BMI can put you at a higher risk for certain diseases related to obesity.

Of course, there is a correct way to measure that. Place the measuring tape around your waist, using your navel as a reference point or two inches just above your hip bones. Make sure it's even all around and not too snug. Take a deep breath in and measure just after you exhale. That's the number that you need. There is an increased risk for women with more than 35 inches and for men with more than 40 inches.

If measuring your hip, you want to measure the widest point of your hips while keeping the measuring tape leveled. This is the waist to hip ratio, which is associated with obesity. Keep in mind that if there is a woman that is normal weight but has an abdominal circumference greater than 35 inches, she has increased risks as well.

Obesity patients are at increased risk for high blood pressure, coronary heart disease, stroke, type 2 diabetes, high cholesterol, gall bladder disease, cancer, gynecologic abnormalities, sleep apnea, mental health issues, and death. This list is not inclusive.

Metabolic Syndrome

We can't discuss obesity without talking about metabolic syndrome. This is a group of five conditions that increase your risk of type 2 diabetes, heart disease, and stroke. Metabolic syndrome also increases the risk of fatty build up in the walls of your arteries, or atherosclerosis. If you have three or more metabolic syndrome conditions, your risk significantly increases for serious cardiovascular diseases. All five of these conditions by themselves are risk factors for cardiovascular disease. The five conditions are:

- High blood pressure (>130/85 mmHg) or being on medications for high blood pressure
- High fasting blood glucose (> 100 mg/dL) or being on medication for diabetes
- Large waist circumference (> 45 inches for women and > 40 inches for men)
- High triglycerides (> 150 mg/dL) or taking medication for high triglycerides
- Low high-density lipoproteins, or good cholesterol (< 40 mg/dL for women and < 50 mg/dL for men)

Although I've talked about increased risks for BMI and obesity, body fat does have its benefits. Body fat cushions our vital organs, regulates temperature and healthy metabolism, balances blood sugar, and stores vitamins and energy. Lifestyle changes including diet, exercise, and weight loss of five to ten percent is the treatment plan. This will decrease your risk of obesity-related illnesses.

Obesity Hormones

There are two obesity hormones that should be discussed. One is ghrelin, also known as the hunger hormone, which is released by the stomach when you are fasting or it's time to eat. This triggers the brain to crave food and encourages eating. After eating, the ghrelin should decrease and the appetite should go away. In people who are obese, ghrelin only decreases a small amount after eating. The brain thinks you need more food, and this leads to overeating. It increases appetite and prevents fat utilization. Ghrelin opposes the action of leptin.

Eating habits to decrease ghrelin drive include:

- Having lean protein (e.g., tofu, chicken, and fish) to feel fuller for a longer period
- Having smaller meals
- Consuming "good fats" (e.g., olive oil and avocado)
- Avoiding sugar or high-fructose corn syrup

- Decreasing stress
- Getting eight hours of sleep
- Getting adequate exercise
- Staying well hydrated

The second hormone is leptin, which is released when your fat cells that sends a signal to your brain to stop eating and start burning fat for energy. The more fat cells are present, the more leptin is released. This leads to leptin resistance and the brain sending more messages to eat, worsening the cycle.

Eating habits to decrease leptin drive include:

- Not consuming added sugar
- Consuming healthy fats (e.g., fish, olive oil, and avocado)
- Getting eight to ten hours of sleep
- Getting adequate exercise

The habits needed for ghrelin and leptin improvement are very similar.

Medications and Weight Gain

There are medications that are known to contribute to weight gain due to:
- Stimulation of appetite
- Stimulation of fat storage

- Slowed metabolism
- Fluid retention
- Impaired exercise tolerance

Because of the possibility of weight gain and risks of causing other illnesses related to obesity, your physician may decide on an alternative medication if possible. The risks and benefits of one medication over another should be discussed. These medications can include:

- Anti-depressants, anti-anxiety drugs, and mood stabilizers
- Antipsychotics
- Diabetes
- Steroids, including corticosteroids, birth control, and chemotherapy
- Anticonvulsants, anti-migraine medications, and neuropathic pain medications
- Opioids
- Anti-hypertension medications
- Antihistamines

Assessment of Weight Loss

Six months of therapy is a practical amount of time to accomplish ten percent reduction in body fat. That's one to two pounds per week. This can be based on your basal metabolic rate (BMR), which is unique to you. BMR is calculated using your weight, age, gender, and health. It decreases with age because of reduction of muscle mass. Because of that, we tend to gain weight as we age and get an increase in central obesity.

Mifflin St Jeor BMR Calculation

Female BMR = (10 x weight in kg) + (6.25 x height in cm) − (5 x age in years) − 161

You can easily find a BMR calculator online and punch in the numbers.

Have you heard about someone who has a fast or slow metabolism? The person with fast metabolism burns through food and is less likely to gain weight. The person with slower metabolism is seen as potentially eating less food and gaining weight. BMR is an energy requirement for basic body functions like breathing, digestion, and temperature regulation. It's what happens behind the curtain during a show or under the hood of the car. BMR calculates what energy is needed at rest. It is the fuel for the energy and is measured in calories. BMR varies in each person and is necessary to keep you alive. Muscles burn more calories at rest than fat, so your BMR would be higher if you have muscles verses fat. Just knowing your BMR will stop you from cutting out your daily nutrients to lose weight. I'll pivot right there because weight loss is so much more than calories in and calories out. Other factors include lifestyle changes, such as meditation, mindset, affirmation, and journaling as discussed in the Wellness Check chapter.

CHAPTER 5

Releasing the Weight

Before we talk about releasing the physical weight, let's start with the emotional boulders we often carry. Because physical and emotional wellbeing are almost always connected, it's critical to tackle both of them when making overall changes in our lives. Emotional baggage can manifest as physical baggage. If you're holding onto past traumas and hurtful memories, then the physical weight won't budge no matter how many salads you eat or miles you run. Many times, emotional eating is the culprit behind obesity because we use food as both a comfort when we're feeling angry, sad, or depressed and as a reward when we're happy. And let's face it, food and drink are a part of our social culture. From happy hours with coworkers to romantic dinners with a significant other, food is part of our entertainment, pleasure, and enjoyment, not just something we consume for nutritional value. Unfortunately, too much of a good thing is what always gets us in trouble. Even as we develop and adopt a healthier phenomenal lifestyle, we may still wish to indulge in appetizers and drinks with friends or a romantic dinner with a special someone. However, as we discover ways to manage our emotions without overeating or overindulging in calories, fat, alcohol, and other vices, we are going to begin to have better control over our consumption so that it doesn't disrupt or alter our commitment to a healthier phenomenal lifestyle.

Emotional weight wears you down. You cannot bury it, hide it, or ignore the excessive baggage that is weighing you down. Dealing with it is the only way to actually get rid of it, but it's not going to be a quick and easy fix. Emotional baggage can be very heavy. You started with a carry-on, and now you have a suitcase and several trunks. It's time to throw the baggage out of your mind, out of your body, and out of your soul. There is a cost for carrying around heavy baggage to your emotions, your health, and your life. But one might ask, "How do we even begin to do this?" The first step is to identify and acknowledge that the baggage is there.

Some people deal with emotional luggage by finding fault with others around them, rather than looking within themselves. This a defense mechanism used to protect yourself. Seeing all the toxic behaviors and patterns in others without accepting the imperfections and flaws in oneself is definitely a form of emotional baggage. The negativity will affect and ultimately slow down your progress in life, impact your perspective, and steal your *joy*. As Tony Robbins says, "Change happens when the pain of staying the same is greater than the pain of changing."

Carrying extra baggage is not your fault alone, but you cannot fix someone else. The solution is to fix yourself and let the others who have contributed to your heavy load check their own luggage. Fixing yourself is a lifetime of work, which gives you no time to fix someone else. Clean your own house before you try to help someone else clean theirs.

Stress and Obesity

Within seconds of elevation in stress levels, the sympathetic nervous system kicks in with fight or flight. There is increase in heart rate and glucose into the blood stream to give you an emergent energy boost and a release of cortisol. This increases the stimulation of food intake (high amounts of sugar and fat) and insulin resistance (alters glucose breakdown and storage thereby increasing risk of diabetes) and decreases brain sensitivity to leptin as previously discussed in Chapter 4. Sleep plays a significant role in weight gain. When you are not getting adequate sleep, you produce less leptin but more ghrelin, once again resulting in weight gain. The obesity and stress over time create a vicious cycle and amplify each other, leading to weight gain and increased BMI and waist circumference as your metabolism decreases.

In October, during my second year of residency after my diagnosis of Sjogren's, I was placed on a large amount of prednisone, which is a steroid, to reverse organ failure. When discharged, I took prednisone for an extended period of time. Eventually the prednisone was tapered while an immunosuppressant was started. Prednisone saved my life, but the side effects I experienced were serious. Within two months, I gained seventy pounds, went up five dress sizes, and was unrecognizable to some friends and coworkers. You might ask me how I knew it was within two months. On Christmas Day, my mom had a ruptured brain aneurysm at the dinner table and my dad was on home hospice with metastatic lung cancer and stopped breathing.

One week later, I had to buy something to wear to wear to my dad's funeral. Surprised and in denial of my dress size, I was afraid to get on a scale. The amount of my weight gain was a surprise and everything I wore was stretchy and oversized. My skin was so tight that I had stretch marks similar to my pregnant patients, but I wasn't pregnant! While eating breakfast, I thought about the snack before and what I was eating for lunch. While eating lunch I thought about the snack before and what I was eating for dinner. While eating dinner I thought about the sweet snack I'd eat before bed. I had to have warmed sweet potato or apple pie with butter pecan ice cream on top. At bedtime I was so uncomfortable with abdominal distension and gastric reflux, but medications weren't working. I asked myself why I had eaten like that? I felt like the prednisone had taken over my mind. Never being a snacker or sweet eater, this was all new to me. The prednisone gave me insomnia, so there was no reset at bedtime, and I had to take a sleeping pill. To say the least, I was stressed. My dad passed away, my mom had surgery for a ruptured brain aneurysm, I had a new diagnosis and was told I may not finish residency. I had fallen into the vicious cycle.

Now that we're being transparent and ready to release some real weight, ask yourself the following questions:

- What are some of the areas of your life where the burden has become heavy?
- What baggage do you need to release?
- Do you struggle with procrastination or unforgiveness?
- What about gossip, envy, or simply a poor self-image and lack of self-worth?
- Are you in an unfulfilling job or relationship that is draining the life out of you?
- What about depression and/or anxiety?

- Do you have a secret or something that you've felt the need to conceal because you are embarrassed or ashamed?

I can assure you that as soon as you're able to come to grips with what is weighing you down, the sooner you'll be able to release it so that you can be the fit and phenomenal woman you were always meant to be. As you begin to shed the weight (both literally and figuratively) don't be surprised when others aren't celebrating your victories along with you. Some who are in your circle might not necessarily be in your corner. We'll talk more in depth about those people in Chapter 10. But do not be discouraged if you notice the cheers and support start to diminish as you begin to evolve.

Some people in your life are for a season, and now that season may be up. There are a lot of lessons to be learned in the transitioning seasons. When winter turns to spring, we shed heavy clothing as the season gets too hot. Sometimes people enter our lives to make us better, but not in the way we expect or hope. As the seasons shift in our lives and we start to shed some layers emotionally as well as physically, we might begin to learn very quickly who was meant to move on with us into the next season as well as who is not meant to join us. And it's not all a bad thing. Seasons change. People change. Jobs change. Circumstances change. Take advantage of the gifts each season brings as well as the relationships, the people, the opportunities, and the lessons. The winter, for example, can be looked at as a time of hibernation, of being in a dormant state. After winter comes spring. It's a time of renewal—time to wake up, shed all negativity, and walk into the light of a better life.

Once you've begun the work of releasing the emotional weight, you can begin focusing on the physical. You can absolutely do the work simultaneously. At the point you're made aware of the emotional baggage, part of the work of releasing it can be through your physical workouts. This will be of particular benefit to those who struggle with emotional eating by learning to replace one bad habit with a healthier one. Accomplishing our fitness goals reminds us that we're strong, capable, and resilient. Exercise boosts your self-confidence, relieves anxiety and stress, gives you more energy, helps regulate your sleep cycle, reduces your perception of pain, and more. This is because of the production of your body's natural pain reliever—chemicals called endorphins—which bind to receptors in your brain, in turn contributing to all the above. Endorphins are also released with meditation, laughing, dancing, playing music, and getting acupuncture, to name a few activities.

Stress can be managed through changes in mindset, motivation, emotional wellness, affirmations, meditation, and accountability. This will be discussed more in Chapter 7.

Signs of depression include:

- Loss of interest or pleasure in daily living and/or activities once enjoyed, such as hobbies, sports, or sex
- Anger, frustration, or irritability
- Sleep problems: trouble falling asleep and/or staying asleep (insomnia) or sleeping too much
- Fatigue and lack of energy
- Restlessness
- Trouble concentrating or making decisions
- Feeling of guilt or worthlessness
- Losing or gaining a lot of weight

Stress can factor into anxiety, depression, and mental disorders, and you should seek medical assistance for evaluation.

Sleep

Sleep is absolutely crucial for overall good health and obesity. Picture going to sleep and punching in, but not for work. This is your reset button. There are four stages to sleep. The first three are non-rapid eye movement (NREM). These stages involve a decrease of your heart rate, body temperature, and breathing rate. The fourth stage, rapid eye movement (REM), occurs about ninety minutes after falling asleep. Your body becomes relaxed and even immobilized, breathing is more irregular and faster, your eyes move rapidly, and you dream. This is the restoration phase when emotional memories are processed and stored and is an important stage for learning. After a full sleep cycle is complete, it is repeated until you wake up. During REM sleep, you can fight off infections and build up your immunity.

Seven to nine hours of sleep is the goal and on average should not interrupt your active daily living. The problem occurs when your sleeping pattern changes. You sleep lighter and your quality of sleep decreases. Quality and quantity of sleep are just as important. Your body actually has a natural sleep-wake cycle or circadian rhythm that allows you to hit that reset button. This is a key player linked to when and what you eat. In response to light, melatonin is suppressed, and you are wakeful during the day. At night, melatonin increases and promotes sleep then peaking around 3:00 to 4:00 am.

Being sleep deprived, the amount of sleep you need increases. Your metabolism actually decreases during sleep, reaching its lowest in the morning. There is an association between lack of sleep and increase in waist circumference and weight gain. Remember the hormones that we talked about before in Chapter 4, leptin and ghrelin, increase hunger of high-calorie foods and in turn contribute to weight gain. This lack of sleep may endorse overeating, change the regulation of glucose, contribute to insulin resistance during the early stages of sleep, increase cortisol and inflammation, and alter the immune response. When you have lack of sleep, you are fatigued during the day, which decreases your ability to exercise. Regular exercise can improve your quality and quantity of exercise.

There are certain health conditions that can cause alterations in quality and quantity of sleep, leading to sleep deprivation. Check with your doctor if you have a chronic pain disorder, depression/anxiety, stroke, or stress or are taking certain medications, illicit drugs, or marijuana. These can be associated with less REM sleep.

Obesity can cause obstructive sleep apnea (OSA). This occurs when the tongue falls to the back of the throat and occludes the airway partially or completely. A spouse may see this as snoring or notice that their partner is not breathing periodically while asleep. The quality of sleep is disrupted and can switch from deep sleep to light sleep. This causes hypertension with elevated blood pressure at night that also continues during the day. If untreated, OSA can lead to a heart attack or stroke. People who snore or who do not feel rested when they wake up should be evaluated for sleep apnea and get treatment as needed.

There are changes that can be made during the day to help you to sleep better at night and optimize your weight loss. Sunlight exposure during the day can actually help you to sleep at night as it contributes to the natural sleep-wake cycle. Bright lights get our attention and wake us up, while dark environments help us to sleep. Depending on where you live, you may have to make adjustments during daylight savings. When it's darker in the morning, you will find it harder to wake up. In the evening when it gets dark earlier, you will feel sleepy and tired, but it's barely dinner time. Sleep is more enhanced with exercise during the day. You do not want to eat dinner too late, so set a time by which to eat dinner. In fact, setting a timer to wake and go to bed help with consistency. Alcohol and smoking can affect quality and quantity of sleep and should be avoided prior to sleep. Sometimes caffeine during the day is used as an eye opener, but be careful about using it too late in the day, as you may have difficulty falling asleep. You should try to avoid taking naps during the day because this can interrupt your circadian rhythm and make it difficult to fall asleep at night.

Create a Habit to Get Ready for Bed

Habits are things that we do on a routine bases that become second nature to us. Because sleep is needed to reset and energize us, getting ready for sleep should be a habit. As a child, your parents may have tried to tire you out with exercises and chores at night so you would fall right asleep. Well, as adults, we may not be wired like that anymore. Sometimes we have so much going on that we need time to relax or unwind and let go of our busy day. Everyone is different, so you must choose what makes you the most relaxed. Melatonin and the circadian rhythm are influenced by bright lights, which includes computers, cell phones, television, and room lights. It's best to turn these off to get your most restful sleep about thirty minutes prior to bedtime.

Creating a Sleep-Inducing Bedroom

An essential tip to help fall asleep quickly and easily is to make your bedroom a place of comfort and relaxation. Though this might seem obvious, it's often overlooked, contributing to difficulties getting to sleep and sleeping through the night.

In designing your sleep environment, focus maximizing comfort and minimizing distractions, including with these tips:

- Use a High-Performance Mattress and Pillow: The best mattress for your needs and preferences is vital to making sure that you are comfortable enough to relax. It also ensures, along with the best pillow, that your spine gets proper support to avoid aches and pains.

- Choose Quality Bedding: Your sheets and blankets play a major role in helping your bed feel inviting. Look for bedding that feels comfortable to the touch and that will help maintain a comfortable temperature during the night.
- Avoid Light Disruption: Excess light exposure can throw off your sleep and circadian rhythm. Blackout curtains over your windows or a sleep mask for over your eyes can block light and prevent it from interfering with your rest.
- Cultivate Peace and Quiet: Keeping noise to a minimum is an important part of building a sleep-positive bedroom. If you can't eliminate nearby sources of noise, consider drowning them out with a fan or white noise machine. Earplugs or headphones are another option to stop abrasive sounds from bothering you when you want to sleep.
- Find an Agreeable Temperature: You don't want your bedroom temperature to be a distraction by feeling too hot or too cold. The ideal temperature can vary based on the individual, but most research supports sleeping in a cooler room that is around 65 degrees.
- Introduce Pleasant Aromas: A light scent that you find calming can help ease you into sleep.

> Essential oils with natural aromas, such as lavender, can provide a soothing and fresh smell for your bedroom.

This is where journaling, meditation, and the power of the breath can work wonders. Journaling allows you to be mindful, unwind, and remain in the present. You don't have to try all of these at one time, but start somewhere to get a great night sleep and dream. This is emphasized in my program All In Phenomenally!

"If you talk about it, it's a dream. If you envision it, it's possible. But if you schedule it, it's real."—Anthony Robbins

Weight Bias

Obesity is a disease and chronic illness that carries a lot of baggage, loaded not just with the excess weight, but also with feelings and emotions of shame, denial, anger, guilt, and anxiety. Weight bias has negative effects that discriminate against people who are obese. This happens in different settings—including healthcare, the workplace, and educational settings—and marginalizes people. I want to help women experiencing weight bias know that they are not alone. One of the goals of the Obesity Action Coalition (OAC) is to eliminate the negative stigma associated with obesity by education, becoming your own advocate, self-love, and positive affirmations. It is possible to change lifestyle habits that contribute to obesity. It is not too late to make positive changes in your life no matter what age you are. I also want you to know that you are not alone. With my program, I help women appreciate their life like never before and rid themselves of the negative emotions and habits they have been carrying around for a lifetime. This is done through one-on-one and group phenomenal communities and support strategies.

As a health care professional, I want to help women cope with negative stereotypes, comments, and attitudes directed toward them. It is not easy, but it can be done with your dedication toward a goal of commitment and change.

Changing how you view yourself is an inside-out job, meaning the change begins within first and then it manifests outwardly. The changes you desire to make on the outside will not happen overnight. However, once you begin to make substantial changes in your everyday lifestyle, you'll probably begin to feel a difference emotionally and mentally even before you actually see it physically on the scale or in a mirror. For example, you may work hard for about six weeks and the scale might only show that you've lost one or two pounds. Let's just say you ate clean, drank a lot of water, and maybe even only caved into your cravings once or twice during that whole entire time. Then you start with the comparisons and see that others you know on this same healthy lifestyle journey are reporting losses of ten pounds or more within six weeks. It's so easy to get discouraged when you don't see a physical change the way you expected, but this is not the time to give up or give in. If you made an exceptional effort and gave it all you got, I can assure you that the progress you've made is major. If you were able to stick it out and finish that initial six weeks, you're probably feeling more energized and stronger than when you started. Additionally, you might even notice subtle changes like diminished cravings or clearer skin. Plus, you've reached a milestone and committed to taking the first steps towards a lifestyle change, not a diet. Keep going! You've got this! *Do not quit!*

Menopause

Let's discuss what's often a major plot twist in women's lives.

Menopause is the stage in life when a woman experiences natural changes in reproduction. Many of these changes are hormonal, as the ovarian function comes to a halt. The main change that occurs is the cessation of a menstrual cycle for one year, signaling no longer being in the child-bearing phase of life. The average age of menopause is fifty-one. Sometimes, menopause is preceded by what is known as perimenopause, during which time a woman experience some of the same symptoms indicated in menopause but on a less consistent, milder scale. A woman who is perimenopausal might still have a regular or irregular period.

If you haven't had a menstrual cycle in one year, had surgery to remove your ovaries, undergone chemotherapy or radiation, or taken medications that have permanently stopped your ovaries from working, you're likely a candidate to experience menopause. As you approach menopause, you may have the start of menopausal symptoms. Lifestyle habits can help with the changes occurring in your body while you are going through menopause. Symptoms can include hot flashes, night sweats, mood swings, sleep problems, weight gain, central obesity, difficulty concentrating, vaginal dryness, and decreased libido.

Hysterectomy

In the United States, a hysterectomy is one of the most frequently performed procedures. There is a wide range of reasons why women undergo hysterectomies, including fibroids, endometriosis, adenomyosis, and excessive bleeding, to name a few. It is another factor that might also cause a woman to immediately enter the phase of menopause, depending on how extensive the surgery is. A hysterectomy involves the removal of the uterus and fallopian tubes and possibly the cervix and ovaries. Some doctors find it beneficial to leave a woman's ovaries depending on their age or if there is no increased risk of cancer. When the ovaries are left in place, they will naturally continue to make hormones like estrogen.

If a woman undergoes a hysterectomy where everything is removed (including her ovaries) her doctor might recommend something called hormone replacement therapy (HRT), which does exactly as it sounds and replaces the natural female hormones that will no longer be produced post-hysterectomy. Some women have had a hysterectomy as more of a lifesaving procedure due to cancerous cells detected. Many women who have undergone hysterectomies also combat challenges and symptoms that might cause weight gain and other issues.

Some women may look at themselves during these various stages of life and think "I am a hot mess," but you really aren't! During menopause, perimenopause, or post-hysterectomy, some women go through a period of depression because of feeling like their youthful days are far behind. That does not have to be true. In fact, if you do the work, you'll realize that your life has just begun. Although you can't reverse the hands of time and go back to a woman in your twenties, there is still so much life to live and enjoy. It's never too late for a new beginning. Many women start new careers, relationships, and a whole new life in their later years. You must stay positive, and as for your physical symptoms, we can treat and/or manage them one by one.

Exercise can relieve some of the stress, boost your confidence and mood, help with weight gain, and improve your quality of life when you have menopausal symptoms. Some people report that they sleep better when exercise is incorporated on a consistent basis. Other menopausal symptoms such as hot flashes, fatigue, and mood swings can be alleviated with yoga and meditation. Hydration is necessary and something that we all need no matter the age. Eight glasses of water per day or two thirds your body weight will keep you hydrated.

When you are menopausal, you will have loss of muscle mass and weight gain. Thirty minutes of exercise five days a week will work to help combat some of the muscle loss and will keep the weight off. The key is to move more and sit less throughout the day. Aerobic exercise and weight or resistance band training help to build muscle. When you hit menopause, you no longer have the estrogen that you need to strengthen your bones. Strength training with dumb bells or kettle bells helps to build that muscle mass and burn fat. Women who do moderate to vigorous activity throughout the week not only get healthier but get the health benefits.

Osteoporosis

In postmenopausal women, there is a much higher risk of weakening of bones due to hormonal changes that come with age as well as deficiencies in calcium and vitamin D, so you've got to keep moving. If you are not the one who likes to do vigorous activity, you can always try to do something you enjoy, like dancing, skating, or swimming, and still burn calories. Select something that is obtainable and realistic yet fun! That way, you won't get bored or see it as a mundane chore, but rather something you look forward to. It's always great to have an accountability partner, and the two of you can stay motivated and do these exercises together. Here's quick tip in the form of an acronym to help you stay FIT!

- F – it should be **F**un
- I – it should **I**ncrease the heart rate
- T – invest in the **T**ime to do it

Even if you start off with only ten to fifteen minutes a day and build up from there, it will be time well spent.

There are so many reasons and benefits I can provide to motivate and encourage you to stay active and fit. Managing one's weight isn't just about looking good on the outside but also helping to prevent more serious ailments, diseases, and complications that increase as a risk of obesity.

According to the CDC, being obese and overweight have been associated with about 40 percent of all cancers. The CDC lists thirteen cancers that are associated with overweight and obesity: meningioma, thyroid, breast, uterine, ovarian, liver, upper stomach, gallbladder, pancreatic, colorectal, kidney, multiple myeloma, and adenocarcinoma of the esophagus.

CHAPTER 6

Being More Intentional

Mindset

Mindset is both mental and emotional, and it allows us to live moment to moment in the present. It determines how you are able to persevere through the hills and valleys of life. Mindset allows you to look at situations and determine how to learn from this and move on. Throughout my story, you'll realize that mindset plays a significant role in how I was able to accomplish my goals. If I thought that it was too hard or that it was unnecessary (considering my primary goal for the National Guard was to pay for college), then I wouldn't have made it. Think of your head as a huge projector screen and the thoughts that you have are vividly displayed across that screen like a movie. Not only that, but your words are also projected onto that screen. This includes the words you say to yourself, like "I can" or

"I can't." Every single conversation you have from within comes flashing across that screen to create a mindset. The reality is that your mindset literally shapes your entire life, but whether it does so positively or negatively is going to be up to you. Mindset means being vulnerable to love yourself and being able to grow from what you've learned.

Having a positive mindset means approaching challenges and other people with an open outlook. It's seeing the glass half full instead of half empty and making the best out of every situation. It involves living in the moment and having the integrity to do what you're supposed to do when no one else is watching. Mindset is the foundation of resiliency, which allows you to bounce back from mistakes and setbacks and come out a better person. It increases gratitude, reminds you not taking things for granted, and allows you to give whatever comes your way a try. My grandmother would say, "Nothing beats a failure but a try!"

Sometimes if we become too accustomed to having a toxic mindset, it can be challenging to reverse this, but please understand that it is not impossible and never too late to develop a new mindset.

If you're like many of us, you've been on some type of diet in your lifetime to lose excess weight. With some weight loss programs, it is suggested to write down and track all the meals, snacks, and drinks we consume on an average day. The purpose of taking such a detailed inventory is not to make us feel bad or guilty in any way but to help us to identify unhealthy eating habits. We can replace them with better ones, ideally habits that will help us to not only lose the weight but keep it off. What if we did that with our thoughts and our mind? Instead of writing down what we eat, we'd be jotting down some of our thoughts throughout the course of the day. Are the thoughts in our head angry or happy, non-productive or productive, negative or positive?

Negative: "I don't have enough time."

Phenomenal: "Let me adjust my schedule so I can make the time."

Negative: "It's too late! I've been like this my whole life. I am too old for change."

Phenomenal: "It is never too late to accomplish my goals. I will dream big, and I will live my best life!"

Do you know how much power resides in our words? You can talk yourself out of many beautiful blessings and then sit back and complain about all the missed opportunities, or you can choose to speak life. The choice is yours. However, I would hope that you would choose to speak only those things that edify, uplift, empower, affirm, and shape the life you want.

We can't talk about mindset without discussing gratitude or appreciating your blessing. Think about something that you've been through that you never thought you would overcome. Something that makes you appreciate simple things that you have taken for granted but can't see yourself being without. This will enable you to focus on limitless opportunities, making you more positive and amplifying your gratefulness. In embracing your new mindset, you will find yourself smiling more often, complimenting others, and giving more than you expect in return. It really gives you a more positive outlook on life, even when things are not going your way. You can see that there is a light at the end of the tunnel. So, stop looking back. Look forward to all of the wonderful things to come.

Motivation

Motivation is what started you on this journey, and the persistence and fierceness of how you accomplish it is your *why*. Do you have a problem or a challenge? Set a goal and be specific with it. If you have more than one goal, arrange them in order of importance and focus on one at a time until each is achieved or until the positive habit is formed. I have found that when you jump from one goal to another, you never finish one. That's why some believe that there is no such thing as multi-tasking since you can technically only do one thing at a time. When you try to add to many things to your plate without finishing one, it can become counterproductive. You will be tired, confused, anxious, and even depressed because you have not finished anything towards your goal. Finishing goals gives you a sense of accomplishment and the fuel necessary to pursue new goals.

It's also important to review your goals. How else will you know and apply the understanding around what worked and what didn't work (and why it didn't work)? If you couldn't exercise each day you planned, ask yourself why. Maybe your exercise sessions are too long. Maybe you need to drop something else from your to-do list, go straight to the gym after work, choose a gym that's closer to home, or work out at home instead. Did you promise yourself a treat and that worked in helping you accomplish the goal? Use that same tactic next time.

Lifestyle changes include an integrated approach to your mindset. Through meditation, affirmations, and journaling, you challenge your inner energy to take care of yourself. You speak every step of your journey into existence. It's always easy to affirm other people, but we must motivate and love ourselves. Take control. It's okay to give yourself credit and pat yourself on the back. No one is perfect, nor is anyone the same. You are unique. Stop comparing yourself.

I tell my clients all the time: Run your own race. Stay in your lane. It is time to find the *you* who is lost or the *you* whom you never knew! Even if you fall, you will get back up. It's like a baby learning how to walk; they don't give up. The baby may need to hold on to something or someone at first, but they'll eventually stand alone. I can inspire you all day long with my story of resilience and faith, but you have to do the work. This step simply cannot be skipped but it is a critical part of success that you want to achieve. I want you to have your own story to share someday. With your customized wellness checklist in tow, *you can do it!*

Emotional Wellness

Merriam-Webster defines emotion as a feeling and as a "conscious mental reaction (such as anger or fear) subjectively experienced as strong feeling usually directed toward a specific object and typically accompanied by physiological and behavioral changes in the body."

Wellness is "the quality or state of being in good health." Emotional wellness, according to the University of California, involves "the awareness, understanding, and acceptance of our feelings." The goal here is to actively seek to achieve a lifestyle that promotes wellness. In order to do so, you must really do some deep diving into your own habits and triggers. Emotions are subjective. Pain is, too. What spurs a particular reaction from me might not phase you or it might affect you differently. It's important to be in tune with your emotions. Ask yourself how you feel. The answer might be right in your face, or it could take some time to access. Give it time and space to reveal itself to you, because emotions are the foundation to your emotional wellness. Be honest about the current state of your emotional wellness. Do you hide your feelings, or do you attempt to minimize your feelings so that you can "appear" strong?

In addition to becoming aware of our feelings, we also must strive to do our best to understand and accept them. Here are three steps to emotional wellness that I practice with my clients.

EMOTIONAL WELLNESS STEP ONE: AWARENESS

The first step to emotional wellness is to have an awareness of your feelings and start writing them down in your journal. You must be brutally honest with yourself to move on to a better you. No one else is going to see your journal. It is personal and private, like the diary you kept when you were growing up. Ask yourself my number one question: How do I really feel about my life? Answering this question might draw up some feelings that are worth acknowledging. This question may or may not be answered in just a quick sentence or two. Then it may lead to even further probing with questions like "What do I love about my life?" "What do I dislike about my life?" and "What would I change if I could?" This will lay a foundation towards healthy emotional wellness.

EMOTIONAL WELLNESS STEP TWO: UNDERSTANDING

The second step to your emotional wellness is to understand your emotions and feelings and changing these feelings from negative to positive. My program will help you learn healthy ways to manage anger, sadness, denial, anxiety, fear, and even depression. We will not be happy every moment of our lives, but we can do our best with what is dealt to us. Life is not easy for anyone—not the poor or the rich—but it can be made easier with how these feelings are managed. Even something like grief can be managed and nurtured in a positive manner. How we manage our emotions will be contingent on our understanding of ourselves, our triggers, and our emotions.

EMOTIONAL WELLNESS STEP THREE: ACCEPTANCE

After becoming aware of your emotions then gaining an understanding around what you're feeling and why you may be feeling that way, the next step is to accept it. Oftentimes, when unwanted emotions like sadness, fear, or even anger surface, our first reaction to suppress it. This has a lot to do with upbringing. Were you allowed to fully express your emotions growing up, or were you told to "fix your face" or "fix your attitude"? The result of repeatedly being told the latter as a child is becoming an adult who struggles to accept the full range of emotions. All our emotions certainly play a significant role in our lives, and if we're open to it, they teach us a lot about what we may not be otherwise aware of.

If you get irritated every time a particular family member or co-worker comes around, then that's your spirit trying to tell you something. That person triggers you in some way, and now it's time to figure out why. If home isn't a place of peace for you, instead of ignoring that feeling and going with the flow, pay more attention to it. It could very well be your cue to make some changes to your environment, including possibly even relocating.

A few different ways that we distract ourselves instead of feeling through our emotions include alcohol, television, social media, or even trying to be super-mom, super-wife, or super-daughter. Of course, no one wants to feel sadness, anger, or guilt all the time, but when you refuse to accept these emotions, you actually make it worse for yourself. Emotions, when understood and accepted, teach us what to avoid and what to approach. Though you hate being lonely, maybe you're not ready for another relationship quite yet. You're still hurting from the last one, but you must sit with that feeling for a while to realize that. Maybe it's time for a career change or a vacation. Accepting your emotions means allowing them to be what they are without needing to criticize them, silence them, or change them. The emotion itself cannot harm you. Certain reactions to emotions can.

Our emotions are the foundation of emotional wellness. Emotional wellness is like a vine planted in soil. If not watered or nourished, the vine will not grow. I help my clients evaluate the soil they are planted in to make a change in their lifestyle for a better, fuller life. A weak, broken, and under-nourished foundation will not thrive. As you know, your emotions affect your physical health. It's all connected. When you suppress emotions long enough, they manifest as physical illnesses. My clients are guided through a series of programs to help them become aware of their feelings, gain an understanding around those feelings, learn to accept them, and then determine how to best release the root cause of the feeling. Surprisingly (or not), it's not always grief that needs to be released. Some people struggle with accepting joy. You'll never know, however, if you don't create the space to assess it.

Affirmations

Affirmations are words or phrases that you speak to bring into existence. They're linked to a new mindset. When I was training for the marathon, I told myself repeatedly, "You are a runner." It's pretty much the same concept as dressing the part. Dress like you already have the job. In the same light, you want to speak it. Claim it for yourself. Start your day with positive affirmations. When I was re-learning how to walk and talk, I told myself, "I can walk the walk and talk the talk." Here are some of my favorite affirmations. Feel free to use them. Post your affirmation(s) on your mirror in your bedroom or bathroom or on your refrigerator and set a reminder to say them out loud:

- I love myself!
- I am a conqueror!
- I am strong!
- I am a survivor!
- I will not give up!
- I am a winner!
- I control my life!
- I am courageous!
- I am blessed!
- I am confident!
- I choose to be happy today!
- I can do anything!
- I am worthy!
- I am healed!

Never Accept Defeat

Battles can be particularly challenging, but the taste of victory is so sweet. We are the masters of our fate. Even if you catch the football, there are tacklers waiting to bring you down. Sidestep them, jump over them, and continue the course. You are not a winner until you cross the finish line.

Many will start a race with good intentions but quickly fizzle out and face the decision (or rather the temptation) to drop out of the race, maybe even more than once, while on the course. It's easy to give up, but one thing winners and conquerors don't do is give up or give in. I am a conqueror, and you can be too by following my plan of lifestyle change to victory. Be the one who will, not the one who won't.

Meditation

Meditation is the act of training of your mind to focus or think deeply. In essence, it is the practice of being mindful of our thoughts. We're so accustomed to multi-tasking. Some might argue that there is no such thing as multi-tasking since we can only finish one task at a time, but that doesn't stop us from adding more and more on a plate that is often already full. Furthermore, we live in a microwave society. Everything changes channels so fast. We scroll social media, going from one person's thought to another then another. In a matter of seconds, you've experienced a handful of different emotions, thoughts, opinions, and intentions. The same holds true with our music and television consumption. Our personal thoughts model that same behavior. On average, we have about forty thoughts per minute. If you suffer from anxiety, you might have even more than that. Did you know that the mind could become cluttered just like a closet full of old junk? A chaotic mind is one that lacks focus and without focus, things just seem to fall apart if we don't regain some control. There are many things in life that we don't have control over, but our thoughts and our own mind don't fall in that category. How do we calm our chaotic minds?

We must learn how to slow down. Meditation is an effective way to do that. There are many different types of meditation but let's keep it simple and split into two types: active and resting meditation. Active meditation is when you're physically active but focusing only on that one thing. So maybe you're washing dishes. Instead of thinking about work or about your annoying aunt, your mind is only on the act of washing those dishes: the temperature of the water, the repetition of scrubbing and rinsing, etc. You could do the same with eating, going for walk, dancing, and anything else you are doing. Running is active meditation for me because once I get started, I am focusing on my breathing and on feeling every step as my foot hits the pavement. My mind is clear, and my center of attention is the run.

On the flip side, there's resting meditation. This is the one we're most familiar with. You're usually sitting with your eyes closed and focused on one thing. You could be focused on your breath, taking deep inhalations and exhalations, sometimes timing the duration and holding your breath. A mantra or affirmation may also be your focus. If starting with twenty minutes feels too long, and you can start with three minutes. It's all beneficial. Besides, some days you might only have three minutes to yourself, so may as well make those moments count, right? Meditation before meltdown could become a good mantra for some, like a timeout for adults that allows you to reset. You'll be surprised at your ability to manage stress if you incorporate just a few minutes of meditation per day. You don't need any special clothing or equipment.

You can meditate at work, at home, in a plane, on a train, or in an automobile. And there's no need to block off huge chunks of time either, especially if you're new to this. Meditation can be done while the kids are down for a nap, on a lunch break at work or school, or whenever is most convenient for you. If you try it and can't seem to settle your thoughts, just go for as long as you can, even if only one minute, but commit to going longer the next time and again the next time. You'll increase your patience and focus, you'll become happier and more content, you'll find yourself less concerned with what happened in the past or what could happen in the future, and you will experience a plethora of physical health benefits as well. One huge benefit for those who might be battling food addiction is that meditation may even be able to help you to redirect your attention off of food and on to something else. A moment of meditation and deep breathing could become a routine replacement behavior as opposed to grabbing some chips or candy. You might be amazed at how focused, controlled, and disciplined you become after practicing meditation. It can also help to lower your blood pressure, increase awareness and creativity, reprogram the way you feel about yourself, and love yourself. Before long, you'll be able to meditate and center your thoughts for longer than just a few minutes, and it will become something you might even look forward to as a part of your daily routine. Meditation is one of my favorite tools to practice with my clients. Try it!

Accountability

Accountability is being nudged to fulfill your tasks or responsibilities. When you're inspired to do something, it makes you want to do it. When you're held accountable, however, you should feel like you must do it. Accountability stems from your own spirit, and it can also come from a support person or a support group.

As adults, and even older teenagers, we are all accountable for our own health. It's your body and it's your choices that you make concerning your body—what you feed it, what thoughts you allow to linger, whether or not you exercise, how you adorn it, and so on. When you truly hold yourself accountable, you'll be able to trust yourself. That's when you can do what you are supposed to do when no one else is around. This is called integrity. This ability to trust yourself is directly linked to motivation and success. That's another reason why it's so important to evaluate why the goal you set for yourself worked or not. Because if you're constantly not meeting your goals, then you'll end up losing trust in yourself. Every time you set a new goal or resolution, the voice in the back of your mind telling you that you can't do it gets louder and louder. On the flip side, if you're following through on your goals, then that voice begins to diminish.

Beyond self-accountability, there are also accountability partners. As you've noticed in my story, my partners have been tremendous in my health journey. From the days of residency when we decided to lose weight together, to my mother reminding me that I'm strong and capable, to my battle buddies running alongside me in a marathon, having accountability partners has been key to my success. Accountability partners can help you stay motivated and advise you on how to get even better. We tend to perform better when we know others are "watching," and the honest feedback they can provide doesn't hurt either.

Accountability is one of the primary benefits of my one-on-one and group coaching program. It forms a community of people who have like challenges. Sometimes hearing or asking questions can help one another. Surround yourself with people with goals like you and gain the integrity that surpasses all. When no one is looking, you're still doing exactly what you're supposed to be doing.

CHAPTER 7

Self-Love: The Change Begins with You

Too many of us simply wake up every morning and go through the motions of the day without considering what we really want, what doesn't feel good, and what might need to be changed. That's because we're on autopilot. We work, pay the bills, tend to our home responsibilities, and do it all again the next day. The only time many of us break is either when take a vacation or when we we're forced to do so. We always have a choice though. That's called being more intentional, which means being more aware and more deliberate in how you spend your most valuable resources (time, money, and energy).

When you become more intentional, you begin living life on your own terms and creating a life that has purpose and meaning. You were not born to just deal with whatever cards were dealt to you. You have options in how you manage it—even if you suffer with chronic illnesses like I do. There are so many chronic illnesses that are linked to nutrition, exercise, and weight gain. Some are genetic, but others are related to your environment, diet, and lifestyle. Hypertension, heart disease, depression, arthritis, cancer, diabetes, and autoimmune diseases are examples. For some women, it's easier to say, "It runs in my family. I'm gonna get it anyway." If that's you, stop it right now. There's power in the tongue. Certain autoimmune diseases actually do run in my family on both sides. I got some, but my sister did not. So, you're not doomed. And even if you are diagnosed, it doesn't have to be a death sentence. However, you have to decide for it not to be.

Being intentional also means looking forward, not backwards. Had my mind stayed in the past, I would have dwelled on the fact that I was intubated and on the things that happened that led up to that. Where's the benefit in that? Where's the progress in that? There is none. There's no point. Leave the past in the past and learn to look into the future and identify what you want your future to look like. There is a lesson to be learned from every failure. Everything that comes your way gives you a testimony that you can share with someone else when they are down and going through something. You never know how many small, seemingly insignificant things that you don't think much about can help someone else who may be going through the same thing.

It is never too late to change your lifestyle. That begins with knowing what you want for yourself. What does the best version of yourself look like? How does that life feel? What are your priorities? How do you spend your time? What does your home look like? Tap into your imagination. See it, feel it, want it, and know that it's possible. Once you've identified what you want out of life, now it's time to figure out how to get there. Having a dream or goal without a plan of action may as well just be daydreaming. Once you have a vision, it will then require execution. This means you must educate yourself.

Even if you were miseducated at some point, including childhood, it's now your responsibility to re-educate yourself. Learn better. Learning never ends, as the latest information and facts are always being introduced. On top of that, our bodies are unique and different from everyone else's. What works for one person might not work for you. Therefore, you have to do the work, through trial and error, to discover what works for you. It's a process that requires a lifelong commitment because what worked in your twenties might not work in your thirties, forties, fifties, and so on, especially when an illness or injury is involved.

A major part of being intentional is being grateful. When your mind slides back to the past, answer it with gratitude. "I'm so grateful I made it through that situation." Then redirect your thoughts. This is the power of meditation. When you're focusing on your mantra or your affirmation or your breath and your thoughts begin to wander, you gently redirect them. The more you practice it, the better you'll be. I love the concept of "yoga off the mat." While practicing yoga or any challenging activity that connects you with your body and your breath, there are certain lessons you learn in the practicing of it. Those lessons aren't just for your work on the mat though. They're life lessons. For instance, when you're running or holding a difficult pose in yoga, it helps to focus on the present instead of how much further you have to go. The same works in your everyday life, too. If you have a goal to lose thirty pounds, it helps to focus on what you're doing today to aid in that goal versus the twenty-eight more pounds you have to go. That can be frustrating and overwhelming. Approach the past with gratitude and approach the future with optimism but spend your time focusing on the right now. Here are some tips to help you be more intentional.

Intentional Tip One: Be More Aware of What You Put in Your Mind and in Your Body

Between television, music, social media, email, verbal conversations, and literature, our minds consume a lot. It's important to monitor what we take in. Take a break from social media and television every now and then. Put your phone and laptop away and get out into nature as often as you can. Be equally mindful of what enters your body. The foods we eat today aren't the same foods we ate as children. There's so much modification, and there are also far more fast food options. What you eat affects your mood and your mindset. When you eat light, you feel light. When you eat heavy, you feel heavy. Your digestive system and other systems are affected, so make choices around what you consume that are aligned with the best version of yourself.

Intentional Tip Two: Do More of What Makes You Happy

If you enjoy traveling, you don't have to wait until your annual vacation to get away. There are jewels in your city. With a little bit of research and planning, I am almost positive that there are some hidden gems that may be right in your area worth exploring. Do you have an appreciation for the arts or history? Maybe there's a museum nearby. Schedule a tour. Or visit a nearby city. What about nature and/or water? Sure, the beaches of Miami or the Caribbean are nice, but you might be able to find something much closer to you. Enjoy a quick getaway that won't require extensive planning or too much money if you're on a tight budget. A park with a waterfall, a lake, or a nearby stream might be within just a few miles, and even if just a bit further out, it could be fun planning a nice overnight trip to sightsee and discover someplace new. Plan a camping trip or hiking excursion to feed your more adventurous outdoor side. Some people take up gardening and find it to be very therapeutic and soothing. Maybe nature and outdoor life isn't your thing, and that's fine too! If you enjoy reading, spend a couple of hours at the library or bookstore this weekend. Read a chapter or two then put it back and read another. You get the point.

Have you ever wanted to learn how to do something like swim, paint, or make jewelry? You can always learn a new skill, and it could be so much fun. Whether you do it alone or decide to enjoy the new adventure with a friend or group of friends, just do it! An online search can show you what type of classes might be offered near you that might be of interest. Community colleges often offer non-credit classes for personal enrichment geared toward those looking to pick up a new skill or enhance what they already know. Have you ever wanted to learn sign language or a foreign language? What about photography or calligraphy? Many of us have had to put our true passions on the backburner due to the usual life circumstances that involve lots of "adulting" and personal obligations.

We've become so accustomed to making a living that we forget to create a life. Unfortunately, many of us spend most of our lives working a job (or multiple jobs) that gives us no fulfillment while doing nothing to nurture our souls. We're no longer invested in our own happiness because we have somehow convinced ourselves that joy and happiness are no longer a priority. It's time to change that. What did you want to be when you were a small child? What was your passion back then? Have you lost touch with your inner child? Not to worry, because most of us do, but just because you're an adult doesn't mean you can't and shouldn't have any enjoyment in life. Playing an instrument or singing might be something you used to enjoy as a child and maybe you long to get back into it because it made you so happy. Maybe your joy will be found in a new hobby or a hidden talent. Reintroduce more joy into your life. This may require saying "no" to make more time and space to do something you enjoy, or it could require you to delegate some of your usual responsibilities. You're worth it, though.

Intentional Tip Three: Become a Better Listener

This definitely requires slowing down. Instead of thinking how you'll respond or even interrupting, you're actively listening. You're giving that person all of your attention. Nod along the way, avoid distractions, and occasionally summarize what you heard to ensure you understood it as they meant it. This makes you a better communicator overall—with others and with yourself too. Being an active listener also helps to minimize confusion and misunderstandings in communication. When you take the time to listen to what others say with their mouths and their bodies, you'll begin to do the same with your own words and actions.

Intentional Tip Four: Adopt a Challenge

This is how you make yourself proud. The Chicago Marathon was a huge challenge for me, but it made me so proud of myself when I finished it. It can be a big thing or a small thing. Challenge yourself to no television and/or social media for a week. That's a great challenge. Challenge yourself to use your journal every night for one week. Choose a challenge that's not too easy but not too hard either, then commit to making yourself proud.

Looking to get fit and challenge yourself simultaneously? Some fitness groups and/or gyms have started doing short-term fitness challenges that can be fun and exciting. Plus, at the end of the challenge, you'll have a sense of accomplishment and pride. Some companies even offer fitness challenges and other wellness perks and activities to their staff and employees. It might be a good idea to revisit some of the things that your current employer may offer at a discount rate or even for free. You can challenge yourself on a solo mission or make it a group endeavor, but either way you choose, make sure that you are challenging yourself in a way that will help you to get closer to your personal best.

Intentional Tip Five: Create Lists

Maybe you have never been a "list" person before, but sometimes writing (or typing) things out in clear bullet points helps to organize not only our thoughts but our entire lives. Creating lists of things like our goals, the tasks we need to complete, and even shopping lists can help us stay on track. Lists can help us make the most of our time and can also help us to stick to things like deadlines and budgets. Do not be ruled by the list, which brings me to the next point.

Intentional Tip Six: Question Your To-Do List

Is all of it necessary? Does it have to be done today? Did you include adequate rest in it? Rest is a significant part of our wellness. Many illnesses are linked to not getting enough sleep and rest. There's a difference between the two. You may not be able to go to sleep on the job, for instance, but you can take two minutes to pause and take some deep breaths. Sometimes it is possible to delegate list items to others if you are overwhelmed. Sometimes your list can be a joint or team effort, but whatever you do, don't forget to include yourself among that list of priorities. You might be able to forgo that full spa weekend planned with the ladies, but your ten minutes of meditation or fifteen minutes devoted to exercise might need to be your priority. Check your to-do list and see what's necessary, what can go, what can wait, and what can be assigned to someone else.

Intentional Tip Seven: Reflect

This might sound contradictory since I said not to dwell in the past, but it's not. Because you're not dwelling there or moping. You're revisiting the past with purpose. Reflecting is how you get out of autopilot. It is how you know when you're on track or not. This is a good time to use your journal. Sit with your values and your priorities and assess how you're fulfilling them (or not). If you're not, ask yourself how you can bring yourself back into alignment.

If you notice a pattern, for example repeating the same mistakes or revisiting a vicious cycle (like losing weight just to regain it all back and then some), then you will be able to pinpoint that something needs to be corrected. This time you're a little bit more in tune and connected with the need for change, and it's utterly impossible to change something that we can't acknowledge first. Some people do not realize that they have a food (or other) addiction until they actually are faced with the brutal truth, and sometimes this will no doubt involve deep reflection. But don't you dare be discouraged. This is all productive and necessary.

Intentional Tip Eight: Release

I won't talk about it too much here because I will address it in the next chapter. However, knowing when to let go and being willing to do so is a sign of wisdom and wellness. That goes for habits, relationships, and material things. Don't just hold on to things for the sake of how long you have had them but rather consider if they add something positive to your life, growth, and development. Be more intentional around what takes up space in your life.

CHAPTER 8

The Way to Go

Mindful Eating

So many of us have busy lifestyles and find ourselves eating in front of a computer screen, while multitasking, or even driving. People who choose mindful eating typically have a goal in mind of feeling healthier, controlling a chronic illness, and/or weight loss. Healthy eating is not difficult, but dieting can confuse you with a healthy diet. Dieting is temporary, but a healthy diet is permanent and long-term. You are less likely to gain weight back when you change and learn to eat healthier. Eating healthier can drastically reduce your chances of heart disease and cancer, which are two of the leading causes of death in women. Mindful eating improves self-acceptance, allows you to improve unhealthy eating patterns, and appreciate your food.

Mindful eating allows you to enjoy the moment-to-moment eating experience, but it starts at the grocery store, as you cook, and when you sit down to eat. You can appreciate the smell and texture (crunch or smoothness of your foods). Every tastebud on your tongue can be excited, and you enjoy eating your food. One key factor is to allow your fork to sit on the table after each bite. Sometimes that fork can get us into trouble and turn into a crank without even knowing it. Give yourself enough time to chew all of the food in your mouth before that next forkful. It helps with digestion and makes food easier to swallow. Slowly enjoy chewing your food and give your brain time to catch up. It may take up to twenty minutes for your brain to register that your stomach is full. When you are no longer feeling hungry, stop eating. Pack it up or discard what's left. It's learning a new habit. It's okay when we slip and fall out of habit and eat too much. Sometimes we may find ourselves trying to figure out why we ate a family size bag of chips and dip, a whole row of cookies, or three pieces of cake. It's okay. Get back up.

Some may really have a specific taste for something. Overeating may otherwise be considered binge eating. Binge eating is the number-one eating disorder in the United States. It's a life-threatening and treatable disorder. It happens when you quickly eat a large amount of food in one sitting and you feel like your eating is out of control. It typically occurs when eating alone and in recurrent episodes and feels uncomfortably full. No one is perfect, and you can dust yourself off and get right back up. You need to realize and acknowledge that there is a problem before it can be fixed. It's just you and you on the inside, and you have to tell yourself it's okay and not judge. You may be stressed and need to walk it back a few steps, but that's okay. Try to think of what was going on before you binged. This is where reflecting comes in. What was your trigger and is there something that you can do to fix it? What type of "diet" were you on? Many times, those fad diets are so strict that you aren't given that wiggle room. If you need help and think you have an eating disorder, you should call the National Eating Disorder Helpline at (800) 931-2237.

Even if those diet plans do produce rapid results, more than likely the weight creeps right back as soon as you resume your normal eating habits. Most diets weren't created to be sustainable for long periods of time. Denying oneself on strict eating plans with no room for cravings or treats often leads to binging, which of course equates to lack of control. Before you know it, the weight has not only returned but has possibly increased from your original starting point. And then the vicious cycle continues.

It's okay to have cravings and eat small amounts of those foods that we crave. Giving in to a craving every now and again is not going to cause your weight to spiral out of control as long as you regain control of your thoughts along with your eating to get back on track. It's important to understand the hows and whys of our eating habits.

- What are you doing when you eat certain foods?
- When you are angry or upset, do you tend to eat certain foods for comfort?
- Are you a late-night snacker?
- Do you have certain cravings during a specific time of month?
- What foods actually make you feel good when you eat them, and which foods actually make you feel guilty after eating?

You'll be surprised to find that some of the foods that appear to be our comfort, our "friends" in time of need, actually make us feel worst after eating. The foods that give us energy and life might not be the ideal choice when our feelings try to rule us, but we can take back control. Most of the time when we overindulge in sweets and foods high in carbohydrates and fats, the thrill is only temporary. I can assure you that when you retrain your mind and taste buds, you are going to be surprised at how things can change.

I've heard some women even say that they never thought they'd be able to give up their favorite foods or that they never imagined going for a cup of fruit and handful of nuts over a candy bar. And as we dive deeper, we might uncover the real root cause behind the cravings. Past trauma, abuse, neglect, depression, and so much more can easily result in poor eating habits. Carefully assess your emotions and your moods that go along with the foods you eat. Then go back to express your feelings through journaling remembering your mindset. It's all a new habit, and it can take some time to make it stick. Healthy eating is a lifestyle.

So where do you go from there? Don't let those foods hang out at home because they will be more of a distraction. Toss them and replace them with the healthy foods for which you've set goals. Healthy foods don't have to be bland. Do your own research online or even seek help and advice within your own network to discover healthier meal and snack options. One thing to remember is that if you buy it at the grocery store, you will eat it. You can't eat something at home if it's not there. Don't fall into thinking you'll only eat a little of the ice cream or cake. It's a distraction.

Remember the new diet can be quite tasty and wake up all of those taste buds. Here's a trick that you can use. When you are at a restaurant and order an entrée, use your tastebuds to track every bit of what's in the recipe.

What do you taste? Then ask the waiter exactly what's in the dish. It's something that you can challenge yourself to go home and cook.

Drinks and Hydration

Pre-workout drinks give you an energy boost. Some are caffeinated, but some are not. People may need to watch their sugar and carb intake, so there are options available to accommodate special dietary restrictions. These drinks help with endurance and make your workouts last longer. I love them because they help with that dragging feeling when you really don't want to exercise but you know you need to. This is especially useful if you exercise in the morning, just when you're getting out of bed. It's also beneficial if you work in the evenings.

Then you have post-workout drinks, which assist with muscle recovery as well as muscle building. Many post-workout drinks consist of glutamine—an amino acid that fuels your white blood cells to help them fight infection and disease. Workout drinks assist with the critical recovery following cardio, resistance training, and even yoga. The drinks can come pre-mixed in liquid form or in powder that you mix with a liquid of your choice.

Protein shakes are a great source of protein after a workout or as a meal replacement. Casein protein is a slow-digesting protein that provides all the essential amino acids your body needs for growth and repair. Other proteins include whey, egg, plant-based rice, soy, and pea. When you exercise, your muscles actually tear. They're microscopic tears yet still cause inflammation and soreness. Protein shakes are a big part of building muscle. This becomes even more important when you age and your muscle turns into fat.

You always hear that it's important to drink water, but do you know why? When the body is dehydrated, it can't remove waste like urine or feces from the body. Water aids in digestion and dissolves waste. The kidneys work by filtering waste and toxins, and your body is able to retain nutrients and electrolytes and improve circulation.

When you don't drink enough water, you may feel bloated, which can also add to your waistline. You will wind up constipated and retaining more fluid if you aren't properly hydrated. If your urine is a light color, you're probably hydrated. If it looks like tea, you're not hydrated. To avoid retaining waste, make sure you're drinking enough water. Water also helps your heart to pump oxygenated blood more effectively to your entire body.

Have you heard that water increases your metabolism? When your metabolism is slow, you tend to gain weight; the opposite happens when your metabolism is high. It's the fuel to the fire, the gas to a car. It's been shown that drinking water before each meal can contribute to more weight loss. Water can also suppress your appetite, so when your stomach is full, it sends a message to the brain to stop eating. Because you are drinking water instead of other beverages that are high in sugar and calories, this also boosts your metabolism.

Drinking enough water is crucial to burning off fat from what you eat as well as from stored fat. Eating a healthy diet and drinking enough water cuts your caloric intake. The current generic recommendation is drinking eight glasses of water per day, which is about two liters. Every weight doesn't require the same amount of water. To be a little more accurate, you should drink in ounces two thirds of your body weight. So, if you are 150 pounds, you would drink one hundred ounces of water each day. Can you see the difference?

Sweating during regular exercise means that you need to drink more water because you are more active. Drink about twelve ounces of water for every thirty minutes of exercise. Water increases the number of calories burned while resting, and it is extremely important when you are working out. It helps your joints, muscles, and connective tissue to work correctly. It also is healthier for your heart and other organs that you need during exercise. When you don't drink enough water, you may wind up with muscle cramping or a Charley horse. When you sweat more, you will need to drink more water. Water also helps to build muscle tone.

You should always drink water when you are thirsty. The thing is, once you are thirsty, you are more than likely to already be dehydrated, so drink enough water to quench your thirst. Signs of dehydration can be constant hunger, difficulty concentrating, a headache, constipation, and not urinating as much as usual. It's hard for your body to tell the difference between being thirsty and being hungry. Instead of grabbing a snack, you can have a glass of water because you may be dehydrated. Drinking more water can get rid of these symptoms and get you hydrated. So, no one says you have to drink water all day, but you can start by replacing some of your caloric and sugary drinks per day and see the difference. Do you dislike the taste of water and struggle with getting in your daily amounts? Try adding lemon, lime, or mint leaves to your water to see if that helps enhance the taste for you. Infused water has become popular too, and I know some people add a variety of fruit to their water to give it some flavor without adding sugar.

Meal Planning

You can do meal planning without meal prepping for the week. Sometimes you want a variety of recipes throughout the week and your "what's for dinner" comes down to what was purchased from the grocery store. The plan includes selecting the recipes and going shopping. It's easier and quicker if you already have a list of things to buy from the store and you are doing this over the weekend. Carefully pick your recipe so you are not making a nine-course meal. Choose for between three and five days for the week. Keep it simple, delicious, and nutritious. Remember to cook with the rainbow. There are so many fruits and vegetables with bright colors that can be mixed together. Organic crops contain higher levels of nutrients such as magnesium, calcium, iron, and phosphorus. These are essential for our immune system and overall health. They have higher levels of antioxidants. Fresh produce can be expensive, but there are things that can be purchased frozen. Your recipes should include things that you know that you like, but try something new every now and then. Remember to grab a few healthy snacks like fruits and vegetables as they are full of vitamins and low in calories and fat.

Meal Prepping

Research has found that when women go on different diets, they eventually gain the weight back and more. I want to teach you how to eat for a lifetime, and not just for a moment. Nutritional eating opposed to "dieting" will help with a lifetime of healthy weight maintenance. One of the best ways to ensure nutritional eating is meal prepping. As you read in the story, I started meal prepping while in residency. I was on a quest to lose weight and regain my health, and the options for sale just weren't going to cut it. So, I started cooking and packing my lunch. You can batch cook, make meals for every day of the week, or prepare the ingredients so you can cut everything up at the same time.

By now, you might've heard about meal prepping. It's often done in stacked jars, which is a great option. I used containers that separated my foods, however. You can find very inexpensive containers with separate compartments in many stores that sell them in packs ideally for several days if not a whole week's worth of meals. There are even smaller containers for healthy snacks like fruit and nuts. In addition to helping you watch what you eat, meal prepping also saves you time (and can also save you money)! When I work with my clients, I learn how their schedule is set up and what days, if any, they want to let themselves off the hook. For instance, my work week was Monday through Friday. I'd relax my diet on the weekends. Once the schedule is determined, then you can set the day to do your shopping and prepping.

I usually sit down on Sundays and put all my meals together that will last me through my work week, and then I'll eat whatever I want on weekends. Let's say my meat is grilled chicken. For Monday and Tuesday, I might have grilled chicken, quinoa, and asparagus. Wednesday and Thursday, I might have grilled chicken over a salad.

On Friday, I might have a chicken wrap. There are so many kinds of wraps these days, by the way. There are spinach wraps and even egg wraps. If you're limiting your carbohydrates, like me, then you'll want to steer clear of the flour and corn wraps. Some people even use lettuce as wraps, and nowadays there are so many options available to those who are trying to limit carbs. You have to be creative, though, so you don't feel like you're eating the same meal every single day (unless you don't mind that). The more bored you are, the more prone you are to getting off track.

If the mere thought of meal prepping seems boring and tasteless, that's because you aren't making it exciting. Get creative! There are so many different seasonings and spices that if you chose to eat nothing but chicken, you could probably have a different variation every day of the week without boring your taste buds. Look up new recipes or sauces to try with your meals. Sometimes I would do buffalo sauce, a peanut sauce, a curry, or a pesto. There are hundreds of different kinds of sauces that will jazz up any dish. Do you like it spicy and hot? Or maybe a little sweat and sour is more what your palate prefers. There are probably some flavors that you may not have even tried before so maybe this is a suitable time to take your taste buds on a little journey.

You can even diversify your taste buds by adding cuisine from diverse cultures like Indian and Thai with your very own creative twist. In this day and information age, we can have any recipe we want right at our fingertips with the press of a button on our smart phone or other electronic device. Your meals and snacks can be as varied and diverse as you choose but if you're a person who doesn't mind repeating the same meal for days at a time, the choice is yours! The goal here is to simplify things for you so that eating something that is less healthy like fast food or takeout is no longer the more convenient choice. Choose a day, decide what meals you'll prep for however many days you're eating healthy, make a grocery list, purchase your items, then prepare it with some music playing. Dance while cooking. Meditate, journal, or stretch while you wait. Then speak affirmations as you package (or jar) each meal:

- This meal will restore balance in my body.
- This food brings me closer in alignment with my highest self.
- I treat my body with the respect and nourishment it deserves.
- Wellness is a journey, and I'm learning as I go.
- I choose to live and to live more abundantly.
- I forgive myself for not honoring my temple in the past and empower myself going forward.
- I thank my body for all that it does for me.

Dietary Options to Consider

There are many dietary options that work, but they are individualized.

LOW-CARBOHYDRATE DIET

- < 45 percent of calories from carbohydrates
- < 50 grams carbohydrates (ketogenic)
- Health benefits
  o Decreases triglycerides
  o Increases HDL cholesterol

MEDITERRANEAN DIET

- 35-40 percent fat
- Fish, nuts, healthy fats, fruit, vegetables, whole grains, legumes, dairy
- Health Benefits
  o Decreases cardiovascular mortality
  o Decreases type 2 diabetes

PLANT-BASED DIET

- Exclusion of all or most animal proteins
- Protein sources: Soy, legumes, wholes grains, nuts, seeds
- Health Benefits

- Decreases LDL cholesterol and cardiovascular mortality
  - Decreases type 2 diabetes

LOW-FAT DIET

- < 20 percent fat, 55-65 percent carbs, 15 percent protein
- < 10 percent saturated fat
- Health Benefits
  - Lower total cholesterol
  - Lower LDL cholesterol

DASH DIET

- Dietary approach to stop hypertension
- Not intended for weight loss unless caloric intake is restricted
- Health Benefits
  - Decreases blood pressure

Intermittent Fasting is an eating plan that alternates between periods of eating and fasting on a regular schedule. You only eat during that specific time, and the body exhausts its sugar stores. Intermittent fasting helps your body to burn fat. There are many different schedules, and you pick the one that's right for you. For example, you may only eat during an eight-hour period. The rest of the day, you are fasting. When you are eating, you should eat healthy and mindful. During fasting, you can drink black coffee, tea, and zero-calorie beverages. Health benefits include heart health, preventing diabetes and obesity, and boosting working memory.

Exercise

As the old saying goes, "Move it or lose it." When we were younger, we could run, skip, jump, flip, and split, without a single thought of running out of breath or energy. Then we grew older and began to find it less enjoyable to be outside playing and would rather spend our days on our devices playing games, texting, and chatting. Now, as adults, we have work schedules and family obligations, and physical activity is no longer something we make a priority. We might hit the gym with good intentions every now and then, but life happens, and we give in to the idea that we simply don't have enough time or energy to be consistent. With less activity and less range of motion, we lose the ability to do what we once before could do. It's true that your thirty-, forty-, fifty-, or sixty-year-old body can't possibly be expected to do what it could in its youth. However, it's also true that the less active you are, the more likely you'll find pain and limited mobility in your body.

Previously, everyone thought you had to do a lot of cardio with your workouts. Cardio is still very important, but you must do some weight training or resistance to build muscles. Even if you are using your own body weight, you will still build muscles. Maintaining healthy muscle mass is very important. This can be achieved by consuming adequate protein in your normal diet and supplementing with protein shakes, which also increases muscle mass by stimulating muscle protein synthesis. This is definitely a great takeaway from this exercise portion.

Exercise is one of the greatest things you can do for your mind, body, and spirit. Working out burns calories, tones your body for strength and aesthetics, helps you control your weight (and keep it under control), reduces your risk of heart disease and diabetes, helps you manage insulin levels, and encourages a healthier diet. Exercise and proper nutrition often go hand in hand. When you sweat, you crave water, and because you want to further your progress, you're more likely to choose the wrap than the hamburger.

Another huge benefit of exercise is that it is good for your mental health and your brain's health. In fact, exercise is proven to assist people who are grieving because it triggers a release of endorphins, which are hormones created by the pituitary gland and central nervous system to help you deal with stress and reduce feelings of pain. It's a feel-good hormone. That's why you can dread exercise before working out but then feel like you're on top of the world when you're finished. Thank your brain and those endorphins! Exercise also buys you brain power. What I mean by that is that it slows memory loss and dementia. It won't cure it or help to avoid it, but consistent workouts slow the shrinkage of the part of your brain that's involved in memory.

If you're already in your forties, fifties, sixties, or even seventies, don't think it's too late if you aren't active enough. Start from where you are and commit. Something as simple and basic as walking can do wonders for your mind and body once you are consistent. Helping individuals discover how to incorporate physical activity into their lifestyle is one of my favorite parts of my wellness program. I enjoy working with clients to transcend what they didn't even think they were capable of. Too often, we accept lack of flexibility and body aches as part of our age. That's simply not the case. Exercise is a common treatment for chronic pain. It decreases inflammation in the body and, thanks to those endorphins, releases a healthy amount of pleasure. In rehabilitation centers, after patients have been in accidents or hospitalized for certain ailments, physical therapists are often assigned to help with movement, and sometimes this includes various exercises to help build up strength. For some people, exercise is even medicinal.

Only you and your physician can determine what's safe for you to do, so please heed that advice. Once you determine what's safe for your body to do, get busy! As you would with your meals, you want to keep your workouts creative as well. Following is a list of my favorite workouts with a description of each, and suggestions for pre- and post-workout drinks.

ROUTINE ONE: CARDIO

Cardio is your primary source for sweating. It helps burn calories, speeds up your metabolism, and improves your ratio of weight according to your height. Completing cardio regularly helps you maintain your ideal weight. The last thing you want to do is eat right, work out, and lose the weight only to gain it all right back. Things happen that cannot be avoided as it pertains to weight gain and fluctuations, as you read in my story. As much as you can help it, though, you want to set a realistic weight goal, reach it, and maintain it.

The simplest definition of cardio, as defined by Healthline, is "any type of exercise that gets your heart rate up and keeps it up for a prolonged period of time." That means you can dance to an upbeat song in your living room for ten minutes straight, and it would be cardio. You can fast-walk around your job's parking lot or building during the other half of your lunch break, and it counts as cardio. There are many different types of cardio exercise that will help control your blood pressure and strengthen your immune system. Aerobics and running are two of my favorites, but walking is also a good cardio exercise.

Aerobic exercise, according to Cleveland Clinic, "provides cardiovascular conditioning. The term aerobic actually means *with oxygen*, which means that breathing controls the amount of oxygen that can make it to the muscles to help them burn fuel and move." Usually when we hear "aerobics," we think of Zumba, step workouts, and the like. These are fitting examples, but there are so many others. It just depends on your preference and environment. Treadmills and elliptical machines provide aerobics, as well as swimming, cycling, and running.

Walking is one of the best forms of fitness. It's easy to do, and we can pretty much do it anywhere. You can time yourself or choose a particular distance. So maybe you set your intent to walk for twenty minutes, or you decide to walk the block twice. These are easily attainable goals and don't require a gym membership. It's even better for those who haven't exercised in a while and want to ease back into it. This might sound like a silly question, but do you know how to walk? More specifically, do you know how to breathe when you walk? I'm asking because it makes a world of difference.

When you don't breathe correctly while walking, running, or doing any kind of movement, you find yourself out of breath and you tire much faster. Learning to control your breathing improves your endurance, mood, and overall energy levels. Start by inhaling and exhaling through the nose, making sure that the duration of the inhalation matches that of the exhalation. At no point should you be holding your breath. When you inhale, inflate your belly. Allow your lungs to fill up completely and draw your shoulders back as you do. When you exhale, pull your belly button towards your spine. Use your diaphragm to empty your lungs while keeping your spine erect. If you end up short of breath, stop and place your hands over your head. Breathe deeply and evenly, in and out, until your breathing returns to normal. If, on the other hand, you decide to pick up the pace for some speed walking, jogging, or running, switch to mouth breathing keeping with the same inhalation/exhalation rhythm.

If you're physically able to run, I say go for it. Even if you think you hate it, give it another try. Start smart with maybe running to one light post, then walking for three light posts and doing it all over again. It's the perfect way to ensure a good sweat, get your heart rate up, and give your entire body a workout. Treadmills are great options, but getting in a good run outdoors is even better because you add the benefit of sunlight. That goes for any outdoor workout. The sun is a natural antidepressant, you have access to cleaner air (depending on the environment, of course), you burn more calories than you do in air conditioning, and it's free!

Because running is a weight-bearing exercise, you help your body build strong bones, improve your heart health, correct your posture, and maximize your lung capacity. As with all exercises, there are so many nuggets of wisdom involved in running. For instance, if you're focused on how much further you have to go, you'll likely burn out faster. If you, instead, focus on your breathing and your posture, nature, or your music, the run might be a little easier.

There are several types of runs that you can do. For starters, you can run for time or distance. If you're running for time, for instance, then you might see how far you get in twenty minutes or an hour. If you're running for distance, then your goal might be to knock out one mile or ten miles, regardless of how long it might take. Or you might blend the two and see how fast you can run five miles. You have base runs, which are short runs at your own pace. There are long runs, intervals (which mixes jogging and sprinting), recovery runs, and more.

Especially if you're just starting out, you don't want to run every day. Three days in a row is usually a safe start, until you learn what works and doesn't work for your specific body. Running on an incline is more challenging, for example, so three days in a row might be too much in that case. You also want to make sure you're wearing a good running shoe. A good shoe can make a world of difference. You have some that support your arches and some that focus more on supporting your ankles and other joints. Some are super light, and others will make you feel like you're running on a cloud. There are shoes that can blend all of these benefits for you. If you have a store nearby that scans your feet and chooses custom shoes for you, do yourself a favor and check it out. It's worth it!

As with all workouts, you want to make sure that you warm up prior to running, cool down afterwards, and give your muscles a good stretching. Finally, tell yourself that you're a runner. Claim that title. You don't have to run a marathon to be a runner, nor do you need a years-long running history to be one. If you're out there running, then you're a runner. There are plenty of accountability resources available for runners, including running apps on your cellphone and even running groups in your city. Don't be afraid of being the slowest one. Learn the skill level of the group, and if it says beginners are welcome, get out there and run with them!

ROUTINE TWO: RESISTANCE TRAINING

Resistance training, according to Women's Health Magazine, "encompasses any type of exercise in which your muscles have to overcome some sort of oppositional force, whether from equipment (like dumbbells, kettlebells, or resistance bands) or even just your bodyweight." It strengthens your muscles as well as tones them while protecting your joints from injury. The best part about resistance training is that sets the body up to burn calories even when you're resting. There's a huge difference between resistance training and body building, so don't be afraid of bulking up. It won't happen if that's not your intention. Building and strengthening your muscles will, in fact, allow you to burn more fat. Therefore, some people lose more inches and see more visual results in how their clothes fit in comparison to what they might see on the scale. Train those muscles! Weights and resistance bands are the most common types of resistance training.

The two most common types of weights are dumbbells and barbells. There are also kettlebells, medicine balls, tires, and sandbags. I've even seen some people use bookbags with weighted items inside. The point is to grab something a little heavy and work against gravity to stress your muscles which, in turn, makes them stronger. With weightlifting, you want to make sure you learn proper technique, so don't just go to the gym and hop on the equipment. The last thing you want to do is sustain an injury and push back your progress. There's no harm or shame in needing help, and it is always better to be safe than sorry. Read the instructions, watch a YouTube video on it, and ask a staff member for further assistance, if necessary. Make sure you warm up beforehand, as you should with all your workouts. Choose weights heavy enough that you feel the burn but not so heavy that you can't complete ten to twelve repetitions and start slowly. There is no need to compete with anyone or try to prove anything to anyone. Over time, you'll begin to see and feel the results from your workout that you might have been expecting from cardio alone.

I most love resistance bands because they're so cost effective compared to free weights. They're much easier to carry around with you, and you can take them to the park, the backyard, or the gym. They're even portable enough for you to carry on a business trip or vacation so that there's never an excuse to skip your strength training while on the road. These were perfect during the pandemic when gyms weren't safe to use, allowing you to still get that resistance training in. Like free weights, resistance bands still allow you to focus on specific muscle groups at a time. With consistency, you'll notice that your form, balance, and focus will improve. Typically, the thicker the band is, the heavier the resistance. I recommend getting assorted sizes of bands and watching instructional videos on all the many ways that the bands can be used. You will find tons of resistance band exercises that work various parts of the body. Resistance bands might be ideal if heavy equipment seems a bit intimidating at first. It could be a great starting point if you're new to strength training or if it's been a while since you've hit the gym.

ROUTINE THREE: YOGA

Last, but not least, is yoga, which means to "to join." You're joining your breath to your body's movements, which is great practice in learning to breathe effectively in all of your workouts. Yoga offers the body deep stretching while also building your endurance, strength, balance, and flexibility. It also relieves pain and tension in the body. There are so many different types of yoga to practice, including hot yoga. I highly suggest starting off in a class with an instructor to ensure that your posture in the various poses is correct before practicing alone. You'll notice a drastic difference in your mental health. Try it!

CHAPTER 9
Welcome to the Winner's Circle

When I was training for the Chicago Marathon, I had to constantly see myself as a winner. I had to remind myself of the feeling of victory by visualizing it to the point that I could see, touch, taste, and smell the finish line. Additionally, I mentioned previously that I had surrounded myself with other runners and athletes. You may have heard the expression "birds of a feather flock together," and I believe this to be true. If you surround yourself with leaders and visionaries, you're more likely to be positively impacted by their influence. The same holds true in the opposite direction. It is said that some individuals become products of their environment. Additionally, habits like how we eat come directly from our surroundings as children and then transfer into adulthood. Growing up in an abusive environment or one where there was constant lack or poverty can definitely have a negative effect on anyone. Of course, there are those who overcome the odds stacked against them, and, unbelievably, they are able to do so by being in the winner's circle. If you grew up in an unhealthy environment but had a teacher or coach who saw something special in you and decided to take you under their wing, that person was part of your winner's circle. Their role in your development was probably so much more than what either of you imagined. Sometimes all it takes is one person to be a beacon of light, to speak a word of encouragement, or to offer up a prayer, and that gift is what sparked the winner in you to come out and be seen. Winners think differently than everyone else. They see failures as opportunities, and they see losses as either lessons or blessings in disguise.

Many people have heard or even used the phrase "What do you have to lose?" but I will pose the question "What do you have to gain?" When you finally start releasing unhealthy mindsets and habits, what will you gain? After losing the weight, how will that feel and what will you gain from the new you? Will it be an increased awareness of self? Perhaps a healthy dose of confidence and self-esteem? Sometimes it helps to remember your end-goal to stay on track. There may be many detours and distractions that will sabotage your efforts, but that is when you have to remain strong. It can be challenging to remain motivated when you're making changes that will impact your whole life. Some influences, in the form of people, places and things, might not be beneficial to the changes you're trying to make. That's why it's also important to align yourself with a support system.

CHAPTER 10

Who's in Your Corner?

Have you ever seen a boxing or wrestling match and noticed that there were people in the person's corner throughout the entire match? When you, as the contender, get hurt in the ring, you come back to that corner, and those people in your corner are there to encourage you, treat your cuts and bruises, and keep you hydrated. Well, I want you to think about who is in *your* corner as you embark upon this new journey towards the "fit and phenomenal" version of yourself. What I'm actually talking about here is your support system, which is something that is going to prove to be very useful even if it's just one or two people. Earlier on, I mentioned having an accountability partner. That could be one of the people included in what we're going to call your "success corner," and then there might be someone like me, a mentor and guide to help you get to your next level. Speaking of mentors, this is a fantastic way to find support outside of your usual circle. Mentor relationships are mutually beneficial and having a mentor is like having your own personal success coach and accountability partner in one. The qualifications of a mentor will vary based on your goal, but it should be someone who has achieved a goal that you are hoping to also achieve some day. A mentor is someone who is willing to share their wisdom, knowledge, pointers, and maybe even resources to help you succeed. It is possible to have more than one mentor in a person's lifetime. Is there anyone in your life you believe would make a great mentor? Is there someone you've followed on social media who you admire and perhaps don't know personally? Don't be afraid to think outside of the box. You never know who would be willing to mentor you until you ask.

Consequently, it's not unusual for some people to observe that you are distancing yourself from them in some way. Maybe you're no longer available to hang out after work for drinks or you don't go out to lunch with the usual group of coworkers because you're now meal prepping. Maybe your friends don't see you online because you're not on social media as much. Change can be as challenging of an adjustment for those in your life as it is for you. Some will appreciate and maybe become inspired by your commitment towards a new lifestyle. Others won't be as understanding, but you have to continue to stick to your commitment regardless of which way the wind blows.

Sometimes the people who you want to be in your corner might end up being the main ones seemingly trying to sabotage your efforts. You know the ones. That handsome spouse or significant other who keeps bringing you those chocolates and your other favorite sweet treats. Or maybe it's that bff who is always inviting you out to happy hour with the half-price appetizers and drinks. And what about mama? She's always making her Southern fried foods and delicious baked cakes and pies. At this point, you might be wondering, "Are they really the enemy?" The answer is no, but these loved ones might not necessarily be part of your success corner, especially at first, and that is perfectly okay. We talked a bit earlier about habits, and sometimes without even realizing it, the people who genuinely love us become enablers to our poor habits. Because of our emotional attachment, we simply don't want to say no, especially to mom, right? Well, this is a reality we face, and we're definitely going to keep it real. So how do you deal with this pressure and these often seemingly harmless temptations? This is where the importance of having a solid support system will come into play. These individuals will be well aware of your health and wellness goals, and their role in your success corner will be quite different from those of the other people in your life. Your success team will help you get back on track when you've had a stressful week. If you decided to hang out with the ladies and overdid it on the buffalo wings and potato skins, your success corner is there to encourage you not to turn one night of bad eating into a whole week. Your success corner is going to be the ones who meet you at the track or the gym for an early morning workout before that romantic anniversary dinner that evening, and your success corner is going to remind you that even though it's hard to resist mom's cooking, portion control is going to become your best friend, and everyone is happy. Are you beginning to see how this works? No person is an island, and we all need support, but sometimes the people around us aren't immediately on board when we decide to make a change. In fact, many of us are resistant to change. There might be some friction or tension amongst your loved ones at first, so having a success corner helps you to prepare for that. But if the people around you genuinely love you (as I'm sure they do), they'll come around and will be very proud of you for sticking to your goals.

CHAPTER 11

Phenomenally YOU

We have talked a lot about the "fit" component of this book, but now let's talk about what it truly means to be phenomenal. Some synonyms for phenomenal include adjectives like remarkable, extraordinary, and exemplary, just to name a few. However, we might not necessarily describe ourselves using these words because, quite honestly, we might not believe them to be true.

Getting our bodies to align with our thoughts is really going to be the key to becoming "fit and phenomenal." Many times, when we don't feel good about ourselves, it impacts so much more than just our physical bodies. We might be more prone to making bad decisions or settling for less than what we deserve if we don't feel good about ourselves. Realistically, there is only one thing that separates a woman who is phenomenal from one who is not. She believes that she is.

Let's look at some traits of a phenomenal woman, shall we? A phenomenal woman believes that she deserves her heart's desires and is willing to put in the work to make her dreams come true. A phenomenal woman knows her worth and sets a standard for herself in terms of the behaviors and treatment she receives from others. A phenomenal woman knows how to set boundaries and create an ideal balance that promotes a healthy lifestyle, both personally and professionally. A phenomenal woman is teachable, always willing to learn and grow, and once she has reached a certain season in her life, isn't afraid to reach back and pour into the next generation of phenomenal women.

A woman can be fit without being phenomenal and vice versa, but the woman who embodies both is a force to be reckoned with. Can you name and identify some women who you believe to be fit and phenomenal women? Why is it even important to be both? Well, it is obvious that there are a number of health benefits that go hand in hand with being fit. A woman who is phenomenal breaks the generational chains of chronic illnesses for generations and decrease morbidity of her family. Sometimes achieving success goes far beyond the accolades, awards, trophies, and degrees. What we don't always see is the behind-the-scenes effort—the blood, sweat, and tears that go into it. It takes a great deal of physical energy and mental fortitude to be successful in this world. As we progress in life, realizing that things naturally happen to the body as we age, it seems like some of our biggest conflicts are with ourselves and our own bodies. Without being physically fit, you might limit yourself in ways you can't really think about until you realize just how much *more* you can achieve in a healthier state. This is not to say that only fitness models can be phenomenal or even that only thin women can be successful. That is simply not true at all. However, as a woman, you deserve to have it all! And you can!

Conclusion

The number-one question everyone seems to ask when they hear my story is, "How did you come out so mentally strong after all you've gone through?" My answer to this question at first was incomplete because I did not want to, as a medical doctor, show weakness. I would say "with perseverance and my faith," but I want to be as upfront as I can be. I had therapist and a spiritual counselor to help me through the rough times and gain back my mental strength in order to have my physical abilities return and get back my "I can do it!" attitude.

I also have family and friends who have helped and supported me through my journeys. It's important not to have to fight alone. I will be able to help you fight your battles also by becoming able to know that you too can be and are capable of being victorious. I've reached most of my goals. Sometimes it may be necessary to reevaluate and redefine what these goals are and how they are working.

When I am running along the lake, I love to acknowledge other runners on my running path with a thumbs up. It's not much, but it congratulates them and, I hope, encourages them to keep going. I do it so that they feel good about their effort, and it feels just as good to do it, too. While it's true that taking care of our bodies is our responsibility and it's what we're supposed to do, it feels good to be rewarded every now and then—especially after accomplishing a goal that you set for yourself.

We won't always have someone to give us a pat on the back, however, so it's important that we learn to do that for ourselves. On those days that you worked through the sluggish feeling of not wanting to work out, but you do it anyway, pat yourself on the back. Each day becomes easier than the day before until you realize it becomes a new habit you enjoy. I've found when I walk, run, and do other exercise, it is difficult to think of anything else. Try this and see what I mean.

You can congratulate yourself with a day at the spa. Treating yourself doesn't have to be expensive, though, and it shouldn't be too hard to obtain. It could be deciding to snuggle up with a cup of tea and an enjoyable book after a nice long bath instead of your usual shower. Patting yourself on the back is one of the best ways to build your self-confidence. It starts by identifying the wins.

If you finally got out of that toxic relationship, that's worth celebrating. If you landed a job after months or even years of searching, that's worthy. If you paid off your credit card debt, celebrate! Remember, it's all connected. Wellness is spiritual, emotional, physical, social, environmental, financial, goal-oriented, and more. A financial win usually means a little (or a lot) less worry and anxiety. Once that financial goal is accomplished, you might realize you have fewer headaches and restless nights. The same is true for relationships. If it's stressful, then it's affecting your brain, your heart, your nervous system, and so much more. Establishing boundaries and sticking to them may feel awkward initially, but it will eventually feel so liberating. You'll create more space in your spirit for joy and for motivation to accomplish your goals.

Take some time at the end of your day to identify your wins. It might include getting out of bed in the morning (if that was difficult to do, which is sometimes can be), sticking to your meal plan, resting instead of feeling obligated to stay busy, drinking enough water, or going for a walk instead of doing nothing because you didn't feel like going to the gym. Thank yourself and whoever supported you—spiritually or physically.

Being honest with yourself in where you stand in your physical, mental, and emotional health is a significant step in learning who you are. Setting goals and loving yourself more than you critique yourself is another step. As it is with loving a child, self-love isn't always saying yes or falling back. Sometimes it's saying no and pushing yourself to do what's good for you versus what might feel good to you. I hold my clients accountable to this version of self-love.

The accountability factor is one of the chief benefits of allowing me to partner with you in your health journey. I'm right there to talk about your medical history and how life gets in the way of your food and fitness journey. We set goals that are SMART, which means the goals are specific, measurable, attainable, relevant, and time-bound. We celebrate when you win. When you don't, instead of criticizing or judging, we use that as a teaching moment.

I win. That's what I do. I also help other women win—only when they're ready though. I want women who are ready and want to make a commitment to change their life. If you are ready, I am here for you, so let's get started. Consider me a part of your winner's circle and success corner. I would like to collaborate with you to help prevent and decrease the effects of chronic illnesses and reverse the genetic predisposition that needs to be broken. I can guarantee you that the change will bring you to a healthier, longer, active life. So, get up from your desk. Turn off the television. Get up off the sofa.

It's time for a change. The only way you can truly begin your journey to wellness is not by chance, it is by choice. I've found that most women don't even know themselves. It's time to pull out your journal and get to know who you are today. Set up a date with yourself and choose a place of isolation and seclusion. Your first date may be only fifteen minutes and may increase over time. This is a time to getting to know who you are and discovering how you feel about your life. You can't marry someone you don't know and expect to peacefully build a life together. You have to know what you're working with. Get to know yourself, too. Then you have others to point out your blind spots and help you grow. That's what life is all about—learning, loving, and growing—and I'm here to support you in doing just that.

Celebrating the small wins gives you confidence and fuel to keep striving for the graduation day wins and the big accomplishments. One plus is to have an accountability partner or partners. So often, we move through the life tackling one task after another, even if it's a goal. Let's say, for instance, my goal was to become an OB/GYN. In order to do so, I had to graduate from college, then med school, then residency. In between all of that, I was taking tests, passing pop quizzes, and scoring well on essays. Because it's always one thing after the next, it's easy to bypass accomplishments and wait until the big graduation day.

When you're diagnosed with an autoimmune disease or you're told you'll have to take high blood pressure or diabetes medication for the rest of your life, that doesn't have to be your truth. My mantra is "The cure when there is no cure." Your healthy lifestyle is your cure when there is no cure. You are in charge of your wellness, but you don't have to go at it alone.

But seek ye first the kingdom of God, and his righteousness; and all these things shall be added unto you.

—Matthew 6:33 (KJV)

Fellow of the American Board of
Obstetrics and Gynecology (FACOG)

Obesity Medicine Association (OMA)
Member

The Sumaira Foundation

Siegel Rare Neuroimmune Association
(SRNA)

CEO of All In Phenomenally LLC

References

Chapter 4: Breaking the Chains of Obesity

Clinical Guidelines on the Identification, Evaluation and Treatment of Overweight and Obesity in Adults: The Evidence Report

Body Mass Index: Increase Body Fat (Adiposity) Obesity Algorithm®. © 2021 Obesity Medicine Association

Cutoffs for BMI on ROC Curve Analysis From Nevil, A., Metsios, G. The need to redefine age- and gender-specific overweight and obese body mass index cutoff points. Nutr & Diabetes 5, e186 (2015)

Why BMI is a flawed health standard, especially for people of color. Carly Stern, *The Washington Post*, May 5, 2021

Obesity: preventing and managing the global epidemic. Report of a WHO consultation. World Health Organ Tech Rep Ser. 2000; 894():i-xii, 1-253

Popovic V, Leonidas D. Brain somatic cross-talk: ghrelin, leptin and ultimate challengers of obesity, 2005 Feb; 8(1):1-5 NIH

Welcome, A (2017) 'Medications That May Increase Weight' Obesity Medicine Association

El-Sayed Moustafa JS, Froguel P. From obesity genetics to the future of personalized obesity therapy. *Nat Rev Endocrinol* 2013; 9:402-413

Chapter 5: Releasing the Weight

Nicolaides NC, Kyratzi E, Lamprokostopoulou A, Chrousos GP, Charmandari E Neuroimmunomodulation. 2015; 22(1-2):6-19

Vander Valk E, Savas M, Van Rossum E (2018) 'Stress and Obesity: Are There More Susceptible Individuals?' Current Obesity Reports 7:193-203

Greer, S. M., Goldstein, A. N., & Walker, M. P. (2013). The impact of sleep deprivation on food desire in the human brain. Nature communications, 4, 2259

Sharma, S., & Kavuru, M. (2010). Sleep and metabolism: an overview. International journal of endocrinology, 2010, 270832. https://doi.org/10.1155/2010/270832

Suni, E (2021). Healthy Sleep Tips. Sleep Foundation: Creating a Sleep-Induced Bedroom. https://www.sleepfoundation.org/sleep-hygiene/healthy-sleep-tips

Johns Hopkins Medicine [Internet]. Johns Hopkins Medicine; Health Library: Depression; [cited 2018 Oct 1]; [about 3 screens]. Available from : https ://www.hopkinsmedicine.org/healthlibrary/conditions/adult/womens_health/depression_85,p01512

Chapter 8: The Way to Go

Intermittent Fasting: What is it, and how does it work? John Hopkins Medicine https://www.hopkinsmedicine.org/health/wellness-and-prevention/intermittent-fasting-what-is-it-and-how-does-it-work

Nutrition Obesity Medicine Association

About the Author

Kina Peppers, MD, FACOG, is a highly acclaimed obstetrician and gynecologist and the CEO of All In Phenomenally LLC. She also is a retired lieutenant colonel with two tours in Iraq and a Bronze Star. She has made several television appearances, including on *The Doctors* and *Someone You Should Know*.

She earned her medical degree from the Chicago Medical School and, after twenty-four years, returned as the keynote speaker at the White Coat Ceremony. She did her residency in OBGYN at The University of Illinois Medical Center and was chief resident in her fourth year. She enjoys public speaking, yoga, cross fit, and running.

Dr. Kina is a thought leader in the field of women's health and the go-to coach for women who suffer from chronic illnesses. Her mission is to empower women to make lifestyle changes through altering mindset, nutrition, and exercise to improve their physical, mental, and emotional health.

Learn more at www.drkinamd.com

CREATING DISTINCTIVE BOOKS WITH INTENTIONAL RESULTS

We're a collaborative group of creative masterminds with a mission to produce high-quality books to position you for monumental success in the marketplace.

Our professional team of writers, editors, designers, and marketing strategists work closely together to ensure that every detail of your book is a clear representation of the message in your writing.

Want to know more?
Write to us at info@publishyourgift.com
or call (888) 949-6228

Discover great books, exclusive offers, and more at
www.PublishYourGift.com

Connect with us on social media

@publishyourgift

www.ingramcontent.com/pod-product-compliance
Lightning Source LLC
Chambersburg PA
CBHW071849070526
44583CB00016B/1609